D0228100

ENTERTAINMENT TECHNOLOGY PRESS

In taking advantage of the latest in 'print on demand' digital printing techniques, Entertainment Technology Press is approaching book publishing in a very different way. By establishing a wide range of highly specific technical books that can be kept up-to-date in a continuing publishing process, our plan is to cover the entertainment technology sector with a wide range of individual titles.

As will be seen by examining the back cover of this book, the ETP list is divided into various categories so as to allow sufficient room for generic growth and development of each title. To ensure the quality of the books and the success of the project the publishers are building up a team of authors who are practising in and well-respected by the industry. As specialists within a particular field of activity it is anticipated that each author will stay closely involved with 'their' title or titles for an extended period.

All Entertainment Technology Press titles have a dedicated area on the publisher's own website at www.etnow.com where latest information and up-dates can be accessed by purchasers of the books concerned. This additional service is included within the purchase price of all titles.

Readers and prospective authors are invited to submit any ideas and comments they may have on the Entertainment Technology Press series to the Series Editor either by post to the address below or by email to editor@etnow.com.

BURTON COLLEGE

ACC/BC No

T
37702

CLASS No

REI

792

Entertainment Technology Press Ltd
1 Kiln House Yard, Baldock Street, Royston, Hertfordshire SG8 5AY
Tel: +44 (0)1763 247088 Fax: +44 (0)1763 247108

THE ABC OF THEATRE JARGON

Francis Reid

ENTERTAINMENT
TECHNOLOGY PRESS

Reference Series

THE ABC OF
THEATRE JARGON

Francis Reid

Entertainment Technology Press

The ABC of Theatre Jargon

© Francis Reid

A title in continuous publication within the
Entertainment Technology Press Reference Series
Series editor: John Offord

Published by Entertainment Technology Press Ltd
1 Kiln House Yard, Baldock Street, Royston, Hertfordshire SG8 5AY
Internet: www.etnow.com

ISBN: 1 904031 09 9

All rights reserved. No part of this publication may be reproduced in any material form (including photocopying or storing in any medium by electronic means and whether or not transiently or incidentally to some other use of this publication) without the written permission of the copyright holder except in accordance with the provisions of the Copyright, designs and Patents Act 1988. Applications for the copyright holder's written permission to reproduce any part of this publication should be addressed to the publishers.

PROLOGUE

Theatre, like every profession, has adapted the English language to suit its own special needs. So, anyone wishing to work in theatre, do business with it or just understand its mysteries, needs some knowledge of theatrespeak. This glossary explains the common words and phrases that are used in normal conversation between actors, directors, designers, technicians and managers.

All entries represent my own understanding of what the words mean and reflect my own use of them. Although working in theatre for nearly fifty years and trying to teach the subject for nearly as long, I have never undertaken any formal theatre studies. Consequently, it is quite probable that my personal vocabulary has acquired not just minor inaccuracies but major misconceptions. Furthermore, since theatre is a people industry, it is inevitable that some of the entries may be coloured by personal experiences and opinions.

The ETNOW publishing system allows for regular updating. Additional entries and corrections will be posted at the ETNOW website and included in future printings. Consequently, corrections of existing entries and suggestions for new ones are very welcome.

A

Above Upstage, particularly with reference to the relative position of another actor or piece of scenery (as in upstage of).

Absurd, Theatre of the Plays which probe the nature of individuals and society by presenting the more irrational and illogical aspects of human behaviour. Particularly associated with Beckett and Ionesco.

Acoustic Shell Scenery used to increase the suitability of a stage for concerts by focusing the sound towards the audience and enabling each performer to hear themselves and their colleagues. Designed, in particular, to prevent sound being lost in the flytower above the stage.

Act (1) Performing a role in a play. (2) Subdivision of a play. Although primarily a factor in the dramatic structure, the number of acts tends to be influenced by changing fashion in the desirable number of intervals. With current preference for a single interval, new plays tend to be written in two acts. Older four act plays divide easily into two. However, with a drama originally structured in three acts, treating either division as a single interval leads to imbalance, while inserting an artificial break in the second act can damage the structure. (3) Self-contained entertainment by a performer or group of performers presented as part of a variety bill or inserted into a revue or Christmas pantomime.

Act as Known Phrase in standard contracts between Variety Acts and Theatres.

Act Drop A curtain, other than the main house curtain, used at the beginnings and ends of acts. Formerly, a specially painted drop was part of a theatre's equipment. But today, if an act drop is used, it is normally part of the design for a particular production.

Act Tune Music played as introduction to an act of a play in the 'restoration' theatres of seventeenth century London.

Acting Area The area, within the stage setting, where the actor performs.

Acting Edition A published play script which includes detailed stage directions. These are usually based loosely on the first production and are ignored by professional directors.

Actor Strictly speaking an interpreter of male roles in spoken drama but has become a generic term for all performers, irrespective of gender.

Actor Manager A person who carries artistic and financial responsibility for a production company, in addition to playing leading roles in its performances.

Actor Proof A role which is so well written that it will survive considerable miscasting or inadequate acting.

Actor's Studio New York acting workshop founded by Lee Strasberg in the 1940s. Developed the performance style known as Method Acting.

Actress With actor now accepted as a unisex term, actress tends to be restricted to situations where the context is very specifically female.

Adagio A variety act, usually performed by a male/female couple, based on a slow graceful display of balancing, acrobatics and dance.

Adaptation A play made from a novel.

Ad Lib Improvised dialogue, particularly that associated with comedy and with the covering up of problems or mistakes.

Advance (1) Tickets sold to members of the audience booking their seats prior to, i.e. 'in advance' of, the performance rather than 'at the doors' on arrival. (2) The money held by the box office for performances yet to take place.

Advance Booking Seats booked prior to arriving at a theatre for the performance. See **Doors.**

Advance Man Person who visits towns to generate publicity before the arrival of a touring company.

Advert Sheet A curtain painted with commercial advertisements displayed while the audience assembles in a theatre prior to the performance. An obsolete device which is curiously neglected in the current emphasis on sponsorship.

Afterpiece A short single act play, usually a farce, played after the main drama of the evening in Georgian theatres.

Agent A person who manages various aspects of the business affairs of a performer, writer or member of the production team. Contract negotiation is the basic service but most agents help to find work for their clients by suggesting their suitability for particular roles and generally promoting their talents. Agents are remunerated on a percentage basis which is traditionally set at 10%. However, when agents offer a full career management service (known as personal management) a higher percentage may be justified.

Agitprop Agitation propaganda. Drama written and performed to make a political protest. Particularly associated with the development in the 1930s of socialist theatres propagating Marxist philosophies.

Aisle Gangway providing access to the seats in an auditorium. Position and dimensions are subject to regulations framed to ensure rapid evacuation of the theatre in the event of fire. Current thinking does not favour central aisles which tend to divide an audience into two, particularly when viewed by an actor from the stage. See **Continental seating, Rolling in the Aisles.**

Alarum A call to war by trumpets and drums. The stage direction 'Alarums and Excursions' often appears in Elizabethan drama texts.

Aldwych Farce During the 1920s and 30s, London's Aldwych Theatre became associated with a series of successful farces, many written by Ben Travers and performed by a company of specialist farce actors including Robertson Hare and Ralph Lynn. The plots revolved around incredibly complex attempts at matrimonial infidelity. Theses attempts were destined to a failure that was as certain as the inevitability that marks a great tragedy. See **Whitehall Farce.**

Al Fresco Performance in the open air.

Alienation Effect A Bertolt Brecht technique (Verfremdungseffekt) which aims to ensure that audience awareness of the politics or philosophical message of a play is not impaired by emotional involvement. The technique involves emotional detachment by the actors from the characters they are playing and the introduction of various visual devices to ensure that the audience remain objective spectators.

Alive Sometimes just LIVE. Any prop or piece of scenery still to be used or re-used during the remainder of the current performance.

All Star A production description used by publicists to massage performers' egos and to boost the perceived quality of the production in the eyes of the public. Tends to be used when the cast has no stars.

Alternative Theatre Originally known as 'fringe' theatre. Aims to offer an experimental alternative to the more formal mainstream theatre and to create new audiences in the process. The best of these alternative ideas and ideals are continuously absorbed by mainstream theatre, stimulating the emergence of a fresh set of alternatives.

Amateur Person involved in performance as a hobby rather than as a paid job.

Amphitheatre Strictly speaking, as derived from the Roman 'anfiteatro', a large auditorium for spectacular performances, usually in the open air, with an oval performing area surrounded by tiered seating. Sometimes used, loosely but wrongly, for Greek and Roman theatres with 180° seating.

Angel An individual who backs a commercial production by investing money in it.

Angry Young Men A phrase coined by a journalist after the 1956 premiere of John Osborne's 'Look Back in Anger' to describe those who shared Jimmy Porter's frustration with the state of the world and with the theatre which reflected it. These frustrations were further articulated by a group of playwrights associated with the Royal Court Theatre in London.

Another Part of the Forest An old printed stage direction which is still used verbally, in a light hearted way, for a scene with no particularly specific location.

ANTA American National Theatre and Academy. US organisation founded in 1935 to promote theatre, both professional and non-professional.

Appear (1) Perform live rather than on a film or digital recording. (2) Make an entrance.

Applause Expression of pleasure at the quality of a performance, traditionally demonstrated by striking the palms of the hands together.

Approach The viewpoint from which director and production team interpret the script of a play.

Apron Area of stage projecting towards or into the auditorium. In proscenium theatres, the part of the stage (also known as the forestage) in front of the main house curtain.

Arena A large performance space within a high capacity auditorium where the seating almost or totally surrounds the acting area.

Argument The plot of a drama.

Arm's Length The principle of channelling government arts funding through independent organisations in order to avoid possible allegations of political interference in artistic freedom. See **Arts Council.**

Arranger Musician who prepares a score for performance, taking into account such facts as appropriate keys for the vocal range of the singers, instrumentation available in the pit orchestra, underscorings, stings, reprises, play-ons, play-offs and the requirements of dance sequences.

Arras Tapestry curtain, particularly one used to screen the inner stage of an Elizabethan theatre.

Artiste An older term for performer, particularly in variety, adopted in pursuit of respectability.

Artistic Director Person responsible for programme structure and performance standards.

Artistic Failure The development of any art involves experiment and this implies a degree of risk taking which may result in failure. Theatre workers should never be denied the right to occasional failure.

Arts Council Organisation with responsibility for distribution of central government funding for the visual and performing arts. Intended to free funding decisions from political bias by placing them 'at arm's length' from direct government control. The original Arts Council of Great Britain has now been replaced by separate Arts Councils for England, Northern Ireland, Scotland and Wales.

Asbestos Prior to realisation of its toxic dangers, asbestos was used to increase fire resistance of safety curtains. Consequently they were often referred to colloquially as 'the asbestos', especially in the US.

Ashtrays Comedian's word for the boxes, particularly when addressing the audience directly in pantomime.

Aside 'Thinking aloud' words spoken by a character for the benefit of the audience rather than for the other characters in the play.

As Known Contraction of 'Act as Known' (q.v.)

ASM Assistant stage manager.

At Liberty An actor not currently working and available for casting.

At Rise The position of scenery, props and actors at the beginning of the performance.

Attraction Current or forthcoming production.

Audience The people for whom a performance is given. The audience role is not a passive one: they are an integral component of the performance, as acknowledged in the French expression 'assister à'.

Audience Proof A play, or production of a play, which can be depended upon to succeed with any audience even if their initial response is a little slow.

Audition An opportunity to demonstrate performing talent and skills to a potential employer, either in general or in relation to a specific role.

Auditorium The part of the theatre where the audience sit to see and hear the performance. A good auditorium brings the individual audience members together to form a cohesive whole who respond as a group which is more than the sum of its individual parts. Without an audience, the performance is incomplete and has no purpose: this is recognised by the French tradition of referring to the audience as 'assisting' at the performance.

Author The writer of a playscript.

Avant garde 'Advance Guard' - A new movement in the arts. Originally applied to a 1920's French reaction against realistic and literal interpretation of a dramatic text, but now tends to be used as a convenient label for the latest new movement.

B

Back Provide investment capital for a production in the hope of making a profit.

Backcloth (Backdrop) A full width, full height, painted cloth hung at the back of a scene.

Backer Investor in a commercial production.

Backer's Audition A gathering for prospective investors to hear the details of a proposed production. Mostly held for musicals so that some of the numbers can be performed to encourage investment.

Backing (1) The money invested in a commercial production. (2) Scenery behind doors, windows, fireplaces and similar openings.

Back of House A fairly new term, possibly coined by architects, for all those non-public areas not covered by the long established term **Front of House.** Those who work back of house still seem to favour the traditional, but perhaps looser, backstage.

Backstage All the non-audience areas beyond the proscenium.

Balcony A seating area supported on pillars or cantilevered from the walls of an auditorium. See **Circle, Dress Circle, Gallery, Gods, Mezzanine.**

Balcony Stall Occasional term for the front rows of a balcony.

Ballad Opera A musical entertainment with spoken dialogue and short songs based on traditional airs or selected from the work of several composers. 'The Beggars Opera', assembled and arranged by John Gay, was one of the earliest and perhaps the most famous.

Ballerina Female dancer in western classical ballet.

Ballet A dance performance, accompanied by music, where movement rather than speech is the medium of communication. Used particularly to refer to dance where the movement is rooted in the classical traditions of Russia, France and Denmark.

Band Musicians contributing to a stage performance. Traditionally located in an orchestra pit between the front of the stage and the audience.

Band Call A rehearsal of the orchestra alone, or a music (ie non-acting) rehearsal of performers with orchestra. There was a tradition in variety theatres that, as acts arrived at the theatre on a monday morning, they would place their music on the stage beside the footlights. It would then be rehearsed on a first come first served basis, irrespective of the running order of the programme. The Acts did not perform but explained tempo and cues to the conductor while the music was played through.

Bandroom Dressing room for musicians, usually located at understage level for convenient access to the orchestra pit.

Bar Area for refreshment, formerly open only in the half hour before the performance and in the intervals, but now an integral feature of the move towards keeping theatres alive throughout the day.

Bar Bell Electric bells rung before the performance and towards the end of each interval to warn the audience that the performance is about to commence. In Central Europe and Asia the traditional jangling bells have been replaced by a smoother electronic sound, sometimes based on the A=440 pitch to which the instruments tune. Elsewhere, verbal announcements made over loudspeakers have become standard.

Bard, The William Shakespeare.

Bare Stage A design style using minimum furniture, no scenery and the exposed walls of the stage area.

Barker Person who stands in front of the box office shouting the virtues of the production in an endeavour to encourage ticket sales for a performance which is about to commence. A practice originating in circuses and fairgrounds but now, perhaps rather sadly, superseded by more sophisticated publicity methods.

Barnstorm (1) Perform in a primitive theatre contrived in any available building such as a barn. See **Fit-Up.** (2), **Ham.**

Barnstormer An actor gving a brash performance lacking in subtlety.

Barre Horizontal wooden rail used by ballet dancers to support themselves while practising leg movements. Rehearsal room barres are attached to mirrored walls and temporary freestanding barres are often placed on stage for class and for dancers to warm up.

Barring Clause A contract clause preventing a company or variety act from appearing at another theatre within a stipulated distance and time.

Bastard Prompt A stage where the Prompt Corner is located on actor's right rather than left. This is normally only a feature of stages where wing space on the left is particularly tight or where stage right has easier access to the stage door and dressing rooms. In theatres with a bastard prompt, stage left is still called prompt and stage right is O.P. (opposite prompt). Prompt desks in new or refurbished theatres are usually mobile units which can be plugged into sockets on either side to suit the convenience of cueing each particular production.

Beat A measure of the shortest possible variation in timing a line, a move or a cue. The actual length of a beat may vary with the pace of the performance at that particular point but it tends to equate roughly with a short intake of breath.

BECTU Broadcasting Entertainment Cinematographic & Theatre Union. The trade union which represents all personnel in British theatres except musicians (Musicians Union) and actors, directors, designers and stage managers (Equity).

Bedroom Farce Comedy with a plot based on complex and improbable events surrounding efforts to share a bed. In bedroom farce, as in tragedy, failure is inevitable. Indeed, it is part of a whole genre of theatre that has been dubbed 'Theatre of Coitus Interruptus'.

Beginner Actor who is either on stage at the beginning of the play or enters very shortly after.

Beginners Please! The call for all actors involved at the start of the first scene to come to the stage. Usually called by the stage manager five minutes before the anticipated time of 'curtain up' on the performance.

Behind Backstage (i.e. behind the scenes).

Belly Laughs Very funny lines or situations which induce laughter so positive that there is a tendency for the whole body to respond in a physical way that is much deeper than a smile or a titter.

Below Anyone or anything which is downstage (ie nearer the audience) than some other actor or object.

Bench Much of the seating in eighteenth century and early nineteenth century was benches. In many theatres even the boxes had benches with hinged sections for access. Benches remained in many galleries until the middle of the twentieth century and have been revived in some new studio theatres.

Benefit A performance with profits devoted to a cause or person. In early nineteenth century, a benefit was often a contractual perk, particularly for a company's long serving actors.

Bespeak A ninteeenth century form of sponsorship whereby an individual or, more commonly a group, supported a performance by guaranteeing to buy sufficient tickets to meet costs. For some bespeaks the sponsors bought all the tickets and disposed of them by resale or gift. Financial support allowed sponsors to choose plays and influence casting.

Big Name A well known star with potential for high box office sales.

BigTime Involved in major productions. Whereas this big time would ideally include both artistic and commercial success, many people would settle for either depending upon their personal priority.

Bill A poster giving details of a production and its casting.

Billboard Site where theatre posters are displayed.

Billing The order of prominence on posters and other advertising material given to the names of the various people associated with a production. Size and position is determined by negotiation and specified in individual contracts.

Bill Inspector Person employed to visit poster sites to ensure that clean up-to-date posters are being displayed on contracted billboards.

Billing Matter The wording to be printed on posters.

Bill Matter Descriptive phrase printed under the artiste's name on advertising material and in programmes.

Bill Pass Complimentary ticket given in return for displaying advertising material.

Bird Disapproval of a performer's efforts is known as getting the bird. Presumably derived from bird whistling noises made by the audience.

Bit Part A small role.

Biz Business, i.e. action developed out of the dialogue but not included in the dramatist's original script.

Black, Blackout A state of no light whatsoever on the stage.

Black Box A simple experimental space, painted black for neutrality, without any permanently defined space allocated to either actor or audience.

Black Comedy Play where humour is derived from bizarre or tragic situations.

Blackout Sketch A short self-contained comedy scene which ends with a snap (i.e. switched rather than faded) blackout on a laugh line or situation known as the TAG.

Blacks A neutral stage environment defined by black curtains or black scenery flats.

Black Theatre Performance in ultra violet light (often called black light) under which only specially treated materials are visible.

Black Up White performers made up to resemble black skinned people. See **Minstrels.**

Bleachers Tiered castored seating units which compress into a small space to leave a clear floor when required.

Bleed Scene change effected by fading out the scene in front of a gauze while increasing the light on a scene set behind.

Blinder Light shone into the eyes of the audience to blind them while a scene change is taking place.

Blocking Early rehearsal where basic actor movements and groupings are worked out.

Blood and Thunder Melodramatic play utilising every effect likely to instill terror in an audience.

Blue Comedy which exceeds current limits of good taste.

Board (1) The directors who form the management committee of a company. (2) Lighting control desk.

Boards An older term for the stage, as in 'treading the boards'.

Boo An expression of disapproval with perfomance standards, now rare at a play but still occasionally heard in some opera houses.

Book (1) To buy a ticket for a future performance. (2) The words of a musical, particularly the story line rather than the lyrics of the songs. (3) The prompt copy is often referred to as 'the book'. (4) To contract an act or production for a specific date. (5) To fold a pair of hinged scenery flats.

Booking Buying a seat in advance for a forthcoming performance.

Booking Agency An organisation which sells tickets for several theatres, earning commission payment from the theatre, or the buyer, or both.

Booking Office Rarely used alternative to the traditional **Box Office**.

Book Show Light entertainment musical production based on the continuity of a written script rather than on a compilation of individual items.

Booth (1) A temporary performance location, normally situated at a Fair and probably tented. (2) A windowed room at the rear of the auditorium for lighting or sound control desks, follow spots, etc.

Borders Strips of material, which may be neutral or carry a design, hung horizontally above the stage to form a limit to the scene and to mask the technical regions above the performance area.

Born in a Trunk Actors born to show business parents and spending early years on tour so that dressing rooms become more familiar than nurseries.

Boulevard Piece A light weight comedy about flirtations pursued with superficial delicacy.

Bows Acknowledging the applause at the end of a performance (US). See **Curtain Call.**

Box A partitioned section of a balcony with seating for about four to ten people.

Box Office (1) The point of sale for theatre tickets. (2) Income from the sale of tickets.

Box Office Appeal Production which attracts lots of people to buy seats.

Box Office Card A poster, approx 10 x 15 inches, printed on stiff card and provided with a cord for hanging.

Box Office Draw Production which sells lots of seats.

Box Office Poison Performer or playwright for whom people are very reluctant to buy seats.

Box Set Naturalistic setting of a complete room with only the side nearest the audience (the fourth wall) missing. Often includes a ceiling.

Boys See **The Boys**

Bravo! Sometimes **Brava!** Expression of approval shouted by a member of the audience.

Bravura A performing technique based on a confident display of technical brilliance.

Break When one actor, who has been playing with another actor, moves away from close proximity.

Break a Leg! Superstition rules that whereas 'Good Luck!' is an invitation to disaster, expressions of a light hearted wish for a disaster will ensure success.

Break Even Selling just enough seats to cover a production's running costs.

Break Point The level of box office receipts at which a production starts to break even.

Break Up Inability to disguise inner laughter to the extent of momentarily coming out of character. See **Collapse, Corpse.**

Breeches Part Male role which is written to be played by a female.

Brecht German dramatist and director who was probably the strongest single influence on staging theory and practice during the latter half of the twentieth century. Although his prolific writings on the philosophical aspects of drama performance have often been misinterpreted by his more sycophantic followers, his theories have inspired most of today's more imaginative theatre workers. A major factor in the success of Brecht's own productions was his flair for selecting such collaborators as dramaturg Elizabeth Hauptmann, actress Helene Weigel, singer Lotte Lenya, designer Casper Neher and composer Kurt Weill.

Brief Complimentary ticket.

Bring the House Down Loud sustained applause.

Broadway The boulevard which runs diagonally across the grid system of New York's streets and avenues. Between 39th and 57th streets, and in several of the adjacent blocks in these streets, the Broadway theatre district contains the city's major commercial stages. For showbiz glamour, only London's West End is comparable.

Buffo Singer of male comedy roles in opera.

Bumping In/Out See **Get In/Out.**

Bums on seats Maximising the number of tickets sold.

Burlesque (1) A performance which parodies a dramatic or an acting style. (2) A show featuring bawdy humour and scantily clad dancers.

Bus and Truck Touring production specifically designed for short stays, often just one or two nights, in each venue. (Mostly U.S.)

Business (1) The theatre as a whole is often referred to as 'The Business', presumably shortened from 'showbusiness'. (2) The degree of success at the box office i.e. 'How's the business?'. (3) Moves and actions which are added to the script in rehearsal, particularly 'comedy business'.

Busk (1) Improvise, particularly in an emergency. (2) Entertain in the street, particularly people who are queueing in line.

C

Cabaret (1) A performance given to an audience while they drink and dine. The content may vary from light frothy entertainment to biting political satire. (2) The venue where such performances are presented.

Call (1) Notification of a working session (e.g. rehearsal call, band call, etc). (2) Request for actors to come to the stage because their entrances are imminent (formerly given by a call boy, now by dressing room loudspeakers). (3) Acknowledgement of applause (e.g. curtain call).

Call Back An actor invited to return for a second audition as part of the process of narrowing down the casting possibilities for a role.

Call Board Board near the stage door where all notices for the production are posted, including 'calls' for rehearsals and performances.

Call Boy Prior to loud speakers in dressing rooms, the person who knocked on doors to advise actors that their stage appearance was imminent.

Cameo Role A part with few words but providing an opportunity for an actor to establish a complete and interesting character.

Camp A style of exaggerated behaviour particularly associated with the acting profession, although by no means exclusive to it. While it tends to involve male caricature of aspects of stereotyped feminine behaviour, campness is not a male prerogative. Camp behaviour is notable for an apparent absence of sincerity which becomes total in **High Camp**.

Capacity The maximum number of people (seating capacity) or money (cash capacity) that an auditorium will hold.

Capacity House A performance for which every seat, or virtually every seat, has been sold.

Caricature An acting style where behaviour is exaggerated to such an extent that very little reality remains.

Carriage Trade Upmarket audience who automatically book the most expensive seats.

Carry Bear the main responsibility for the success of a production. Expressed in such phrases as 'she carries the show'.

Carry a Scene (1) When a scene is written in such a way that the burden of making it work is centred upon one of the roles. (2) When the general quality of the acting is such that the burden of making a particular scene work falls upon one actor.

Cast (1) Allocating actors to roles. (2) The group of actors selected for a particular production.

Casting Call An audition session to give several actors an opportunity to be considered for a particular role. The call may be 'open' to all comers or it may be restricted to those invited on the suggestion of their agents or a casting director. Open calls have become less frequent following legislation changes which prevent open calls being restricted to Equity trade union members.

Casting Couch Implication that a successful audition might involve rather more than a demonstration of ability to play the part.

Casting Director Person who suggests possibly suitable actors for the director and producer to audition for the various parts.

Casting Directory File of actors with photographs, parts played, special abilities, etc.

Cast List Schedule of all the roles and the names of the actors contracted to play them. A few, limited circulation, copies will include contact information such as agent details, addresses, ex-directory phone numbers, mobiles, etc.

Cat Call A public expression of disappointment with an actor, uttered during a performance.

Catch Phrase A verbal expression with which a particular performer becomes associated. In a few cases, catch phrases have been associated with an actor - for example, Robertson Hare was expected to say "Oh, calamity!" in every Aldwych farce and the audience would have felt cheated by its omission. However, catch phrases are more frequently used by stand-up comedians and by writers of television comedy series.

Cellar The area under the stage from which scenery and actors may appear and into which they may descend.

Censorship A process by which only officially sanctioned scripts may be performed. Abandoned in Britain in 1968.

Centre The mid point of the stage where an occupying actor can command the attention of the audience and the rest of the cast. It is normally on the centre line bisecting the stage from front to back. But the position upstage or downstage on this line will depend on the architecture of the theatre and the geography of the scenery. See **Point of Command.**

Chairman Music Hall compere who sat at a table at the side of the stage and introduced the acts with a verbal flourish.

Chamber Set Scenery which reproduces a room in realistic detail.

Character A role in a play.

Character Actor An actor who specialises in playing supportive roles which are strongly written and whose portrayal makes a strong impression on the audience.

Character Make-Up The use of greasepaint and prosthetics to alter the age and appearance of an actor's face.

Character Part A strongly written supportive role.

Cheat Small changes which (hopefully) are imperceptible to the audience. Virtually everything in a performance can be subjected to cheating from positioning actors to catching up with a missed lighting cue.

Chew the Scenery To act with exaggerated movements and gestures.

Children's Theatre Productions created specifically for a young audience.

Choreographer Originally a person who creates dances but now widened to include anyone devising movement, or responsible for staging musical numbers and sequences.

Chorus (1) Group of actors in classical Greek drama, speaking in unison. (2) Group of singing and dancing actors who provide the crowds in lyric theatre works. Although their music may only have four vocal lines corresponding with soprano, alto, tenor and bass groupings, most of today's directors seek to help chorus members develop individual characterisations.

Christmas Pantomime The theatre form which occupies virtually all British theatres over a two to six weeks season centered on the Christmas and New Year holiday period. Loosely based on traditional fairy stories such as Cinderella, Aladdin or Dick Whittington, the script is expected to embrace old jokes and topical references, with the plot adjusted to exploit particular personal talents of individual actors who often play roles of a quite different type from their normal casting. Tradition, inevitably subject to erosion, requires the hero to be played by a woman (the 'Principal Boy') and the comedy woman played by a man (the 'Dame'). Colourful costumes and spectacular scenery are built to last at least ten seasons. All the family go and it is the introduction to theatre for most children. Although scorned by many serious minded theatregoers, Christmas pantomime survives because its box office success helps many theatres to survive for the rest of the year.

Circle A curving balcony in the auditorium.

Circuit Series of theatres visited by touring companies.

Civic Theatre A theatre building, with or without its own acting ensemble, which is maintained by the local government of a city.

Clap Applaud by striking the palms of the hands together.

Claque Group of audience who are paid to applaud a particular actor.

Class The daily limbering-up call for dancers.

Classic An established play of sufficient literary and dramatic quality to ensure frequent productions. Classics normally, but not necessarily, date from an earlier century.

Clear! Instruction for everyone except the actors involved in the next scene to leave the stage because that scene is about to be revealed.

Close The end of a run ('We close on Saturday').

Close in Ones A variety act structured so that its final sequence could be played downstage, allowing a front cloth to be dropped in, or running tabs closed, so that the next act may be set up behind.

Cloth A scene painted on a large area of vertical canvas. A backcloth completes the rear of a scene while a frontcloth permits scene changing to take place behind while the performance continues in front.

Clothes Costumes worn on stage.

Clown A role, and the actor playing such a role, where the comedy is mainly physical and derived from an apparent simple-mindedness that disguises considerable cunning. Traditional clowns wear costume and make up which have been associated with the role for centuries.

Clown white The traditional foundation make-up worn by circus clowns.

Coach (1) Prepare a performer for a role. (2) The specialist who works with a performer. Coaching is standard in opera but rare in drama.

COBO Ticket awaiting collection at the box office (i.e. 'Care Of the Box Office').

Cod A hoax, leg-pull or send-up - particularly one directed towards a fellow perfomer.

Collapse Overcome by laughter to the extent of being unable to sustain characterisation. Occurs as a result of some private joke or situation which is frequently not understood by the audence. See **Break Up, Corpse.**

Collective Theatre company based on equality in all matters including financial responsibility and reward.

Comeback Performance by an actor who has been absent from the stage for some considerable time.

Comedian A performer who seeks to extract verbal or visual humour from a situation in order to induce laughter in the audience.

Comedien French for all actors (not only comedians).

Comedienne French for actress.

Come down (1) Move towards the front of the stage (**Downstage**) and therefore closer to the audience. (2) The end of the performance (i.e. when the final curtain has come down).

Comedy A play which treats its subject in a not too serious manner and usually has a happy ending. The dialogue tends to be humorous but situations and characters are more realistic than in "farce".

Comedy of Manners A witty comedy which gently satirises the behaviour affectations of a segment of society who are concerned to demonstrate their sophistication.

Comic (1) A comedian. (2) A non-serious performance or situation within a performance which induces smiles and/or laughter.

Comic Relief Comedy scene written into a tragic play to relieve the tension and thereby increase, by contrast, the power of subsequent dramatic events.

Command Performance A performance in aid of charity given under royal patronage with the performers donating their services.

Commedia Dell'Arte A comedy tradition based on stock characters played by masked actors. Developed in 16th to 18th century Italy, performances were originally improvised but gradually acquired sequences of set business. The stock characters became a major influence on opera and their behaviour is so typical of certain standard human behaviour patterns that aspects of commedia dell'arte characters can still be identified in much of today's playwriting.

Commercial Theatre funded by investors who hope that productions will be sufficiently successful at the box office to not only repay their capital investment but to generate sufficiently large profits to compensate for the high risk involved.

Company A team of actors, associated production and administrative staff.

Company Manager The producer's day-to-day link with the acting company and with the management team of the theatre in which the perform-ances are taking place.

Compere A person who provides continuity in a performance by addressing the audience and introducing each indivivdual self-contained act.

Complimentary (Comp) Ticket issued free with the 'compliments' of the theatre management.

Comprimario Member of an opera company playing supporting character roles.

Concert Party A group of entertainers presenting an assortment of songs and sketches, usually with very little or no scenery and few costume changes.

Concessionaire Person or firm with a contract to provide services such as bars and catering.

Conductor The person in musical charge of a performance. The conductor is also usually the musical director with overall responsibility for the musical aspects of the production. However, for a long running musical, there may be a musical director who does not conduct performances but, by means of regular visits, retains a watching brief over the musical standards of the show.

Constructivism A scenographic technique using abstract structures, often skeletal. Popularised by the early 20th century Russian director Meyerhold.

Continental Seating Long rows of seats with no central aisle. The potential emergency escape hazard is compensated by increased distance between rows.

Contour Curtain A curtain with several hoisting lines so that sections may be raised to different heights to produce swagging in alternative scalloped patterns.

Contrived A piece of dramatic writing or acting which lacks plausibility.

Conventions Formalised aspects of a production style which, through consistency of use, are accepted as representing natural behviour in a realistic environment.

Conversation Piece A play where the emphasis is on dialogue and debate rather than action.

Copyright Scripts, music and the work of the director, choreographer and design team are personal intellectual property. The contracts between each member of the production team and the producer include the terms under which the copyright is licensed for performance.

Corner, The See **Prompt Corner.**

Corps De Ballet The chorus in classical dance, performing as an ensemble rather than as individuals.

Corpse Inability to keep a straight face during a performance because of a desire to laugh trigged by some unusual situation.

Corsican Trap A trap with a platform which moves across the stage as it rises so that actors seem to glide across the stage as they appear through it. First used in "The Corsican Brothers". Also known as the Ghost Glide.

Coryphee A member of a ballet company who has been promoted from the Corps de Ballet but does not yet dance principal solo roles.

Co-Star Two or more actors equally sharing the top billing.

Costume (1) The clothes worn by an actor in performance. (2) More specifically, clothes of an earlier period than the present.

Costume Drama A historical play where the actors are dressed in accurate recreations of the clothes of the period.

Costume Shop Workshop where costumes are cut and sewn. When located within a theatre building, often called by the all-embracing 'wardrobe'.

Counterfoil Part of a ticket, often callled a **Stub**, retained by the box-office for accountancy purposes. Increasingly rare as a consequence of the use of computers which record sales information in their software.

Count the House Estimate the number of people in the auditorium and the total value of seats sold. Older actors and actor managers liked to do this (often using a peep hole in the curtain), motivated by curiosity, vanity or suspicion about the honesty of the box office staff.

Coup De Theatre A textual or staging device, usually unexpected and often dramatically showy, upon which the plot develops or is even resolved.

Cover Understudy or standby actor, particularly in opera.

Create a Role The first actor to play a character in a play which subsequently becomes a frequently performed classic.

Credits Acknowledgements in the programme of the contributions made by the personnel involved in the production. Programme credits for suppliers have long been a useful inducement for negotiating discounts.

Crepe Hair Artificial hair, supplied in a tight plait to be combed out and glued to the face when making up.

Crew The technicians responsible for all the stage operations. May be qualified by specialism, ie stage crew, fly crew, LX crew, etc.

Crit Abbreviation of 'criticism', an analytical report published in a newspaper or magazine.

Critic Although applicable to anyone offering qualitative analysis of a work or its performance, normally reserved for journalists writing reviews in newspapers and magazines.

Cross An actor's move across the stage.

Crowd Scene A part of the play which includes many supporting actors.

Cruelty, Theatre of Plays intended to shock the audience into an awareness of underlying savage aspects of society.

Cue (1) The signal that initiates a change of any kind during a performance. (2) A line of dialogue or an action that stimulates a response from another actor.

Curtain A large expanse of hanging fabric use to conceal and reveal action takng place behind. Often used as a contraction when referring to the House Curtain. (Small curtains as used on windows, etc, are usually referred to as **Drapes**.) See **Tabs.**

Curtain Call Acknowledgement of applause, traditionally taken by raising and lowering the house curtain or coming through its central overlapping gap. In the absence of a curtain, the lighting is blacked out and restored several times. Known as Bows in the US.

Curtain Cue The word, music or action which motivates the raising or lowering of the house curtain at the beginning or end of a performance or of a scene within a performance.

Curtain Fall The end of the performance.

Curtain Going Up! Warning from the stage manager to the actors and backstage crew that the curtain is about to rise.

Curtain Line The last words of a scene upon which the curtain is then lowered ('falls').

Curtain Music Music which starts as the houselights dim and then fades away just after the curtain has risen. Very common - virtually standard practice for box set comedies - until the nineteen sixties.

Curtain Raiser A short one act play performed prior to the main play of the evening. Very rare in today's theatre. See **Afterpiece.**

Curtain Speech Thanks spoken by the leading actor at the final curtain call. A custom which has declined although still regularly observed at the end of Christmas pantomimes.

Curtain Time Advertised time of the beginning or end of the performance.

Curtain Up! The beginning of the performance. Originally the raising of the curtain to reveal the stage, but often still used when there is no curtain.

Custard Pie A comedy routine where the victims have a plateful of sticky goo applied to their faces. The mixture is usually a light foam of shaving soap rather than the custard which it resembles. See **Slosh.**

Cuts Dialogue or music removed from a script for a particular production, either to shorten or to make the production more dramatically effective.

Cyclorama Plain cloth extending around and above the stage to give a feeling of infinite space. Permanent cycloramas, plaster surfaced, were a feature of serious theatres in the earlier part of the 20th century, particularly in central Europe where they were curved to wrap around at least the rear and sides of the acting area, and sometimes also domed over the top. The term is often used for a plain skycloth, either straight or with a limited curve at the ends.

D

Dame Comedy woman, usually the mother of the hero, played by a man, in British traditional christmas pantomime. A true dame deliberately avoids any attempt at realistic female impersonation.

Dance Captain Senior member of a group of chorus dancers. Responsible for liasing with the management, maintaining standards and generally mothering.

Dark A theatre which is temporarily or permanently without performances.

Darling Common form of address used by actors and production teams. Subtleties of inflection can reduce its inherent implication of affection.

Date (1) Confirmed booking between a venue and performer or production. (2) A theatre which receives tours.

Day Bill Poster giving detailed information about tonight's performance. Any reference to forthcoming performances, even tomorrow's, is likely to be restricted to a single line announcing the title. Traditional day bills are now rarely seen in the UK and US, but are still common in Italy and some parts of central Europe.

Date Book Specially printed diary or pages in a diary for artists to note their contracted performances.

Dead (1) The height of a piece of suspended scenery (trim in US). (2) Discarded items of scenery. See **Kill.**

Dead Pan Delivery of a line without any facial expression by the actor. A device often used in speaking lines intended to produce a laughter response from the audience.

Dead Segue See Segue.

Dead Spot Part of the auditorium with an inferior acoustic.

Death at the Box Office Prediction that a proposed play or performer will fail to attract an audience.

Debut First appearance by an actor: either the very first of a career or the first in a particular role.

Deck The stage floor. Sometimes confined to a special floor laid as part of the scenic design for a particular production.

Declaim Speak in a formal way with rounded diction, emphasising the words in a considerably more exaggerated manner than normal conversation.

Decor This older word for scenery has been falling into disuse with the growth of the idea that scenic environments should be an integral part of productions rather than just decorative backgrounds. See **Scenography.**

Delivery Manner in which an actor speaks the text.

Denoument The resolution of the plot towards the end of a play when complications are unravelled and details clarified.

Dep Substitute performer who 'deputises', particularly an orchestral musician.

Depth The dimension of a stage or scene from the front edge to the back wall.

Designer Person responsible for conceiving the visual environment of a production and supervising its execution. Separate designers may be employed for scenery, costume and lighting. See **Scenographer.**

Deus Ex Machina (1) The introduction of a god to resolve a dramatic plot. The arrival of such a god usually involved the use of complex stage machinery, frequently portraying a descent from the heavens. (2) Often extended to include an artificial solution of a complicated plot.

Devised A production which has been developed in the rehearsal room through experiment rather than by interpretation of a prepared text.

Dialogue Often used to describe all the text of a playscript although, strictly speaking, it should only refer to talk between two people.

Diamond Horseshoe The glittering first night audience in the first (Grand or Dress) circle.

Diction Speech, particularly its clarity and projection.

Die Failure by an actor or production to be appreciated by an audience.

Die a Death Emphatic failure.

Digs Theatrical landladies, a vanishing breed, were once at the very heart of stage folklore. But lodgings specifically for actors have almost disappeared with the decline in weekly touring dates.

Dinner Theatre Theatre where the auditorium is laid out with tables and the performance is preceded by a meal. When the show is words rather than music, it is likely to be a comedy or whodunnit and probably shortened.

Director The person with ultimate responsibility for interpretation of the script through artistic leadership of the actors and supporting production team.

Discover Revealing a scene or actor to the audience by such devices as raising or drawing curtains, fading lights from blackout or bleeding through gauzes.

Discovered on (at Rise) Scenery or actors positioned on stage so that their presence will be revealed when the curtain rises or the lights are faded up from blackout.

Distress Make clothes or scenery look worn and used.

Diva A female operatic star.

Divertissment Originally a short entertainment between the heavier dramatic acts of a play, but now more generally used for a rather frothy light-weight production.

Dock High ceilinged scenic storage area adjacent to the stage.

Dock doors High doors leading directly to the stage for getting scenery in and out of the theatre.

Doctor See **Play Doctor.**

Doors (1) Seats sold immediately prior to the performance rather than in advance. (2) The total receipts at each performance from such sales.

Double (1) Two characters in a production played by one actor. (2) One actor substituted for another, without the audience being aware, in order to make a trick or stunt possible. (3) A piece of scenery which is used more than once, ie 'doubles' between two scenes.

Double Act Two performers, particularly comedians, who work together as a self-contained entertainment team on the variety stage. One member of the partnership is traditionally a "straight" (wo)man who "feeds" lines to the comic who makes a laugh inducing response. However, many of the great double acts, such as Morecambe and Wise or French and Saunders, are based upon a more balanced equality of partnership.

Double Bill A performance consisting of two separate pieces which are each self-contained but may, ideally, have some thematic link.

Double Cast A production for which two actors have been rehearsed for one, several, or all of the roles. Most likely to occur in opera where the frequency with which a singer can perform is limited by the risk of vocal strain.

Double Take An actor's comedy response where two facial expressions with a pause between them are used to indicate a belated recognition of the significance of a line or action.

Downstage The area of stage nearest to the audience.

Drag (1) Female impersonation by a male actor. (2) The female clothing worn by such a male actor.

Drama Literature in dialogue form, intended primarily to be performed rather than read.

Drama School An educational institution where the syllabus concentrates specifically on detailed professional training rather than a broad academic approach to studying the philosophies and processes of theatre.

Dramatic Anything pertaining to a staged performance, particularly when a considerable degree of emotional intensity is involved.

Dramatic Irony When a character does not know something that the audience does. So there is a contrast between what the character expects to happen and what the audience knows will happen.

Dramatic Rights Permission to adapt a literary work for performance.

Dramatis Personae A cast list, possibly annotated with concisely phrased descriptions of each character and their inter-relationships.

Dramatist Writer of plays. Also known as a **Playwright.**

Dramaturgy The study of play texts with a view to performance. Many theatres employ a Dramaturg who advises on play choice and supports the production team by assisting with research and generally acting as an in-house critic of work in preparation. Dramaturgs are sometimes called Literary Managers.

Draw Performance which attracts an audience.

Drawing Room Comedy A non-serious play about people enjoying a comfortable life style with a few problems which are superficial but amusing.

Dress (1) A dress rehearsal. (2) Adding decorative (i.e. non-functional) items to a stage scenic environment.

Dress Circle The first (i.e. lowest) balcony in a theatre. Name derived from a former expectation that evening dress would be worn in this part of the house.

Dresser While a job description might confine the duties to helping the actor with costume care and costume changing, many dressers fulfil a wide range of roles from secretary through bodyguard to psychotherapist.

Dressing room The actor's personal backstage space which is rather more than just a place to change into stage costume and make-up, especially on a matinee day when the actor may spend more time in the theatre than at home.

Dress Rehearsal A rehearsal with all costumes, props, scenery and lights. See **General.**

Dressing the House Selling seats in such a pattern that the auditorium looks fuller than it actually is.

Dressing the Stage Positioning props and actors to make a balanced picture on the stage.

Drop Scenic cloth lowered or 'dropped' from the flys above the stage. (Particularly US).

Dry Forget the words of the script.

Dry Ice Vapour, heavier than air, forming a mist on the stage floor. Made by adding frozen carbon dioxde to boiling water.

Early Doors Two-tier pricing system used in the days when pit and gallery seating was unreserved benches. Audience prepared to pay a higher price were admitted early to get first choice of the seats. When the gallery queue was short at Edinburgh King's Theatre in the late 1940s and early 1950s, the author recallls waiting until the price came down from one and sixpence (7.5p) to a shilling (5p). Gallery queues are the origin of the old pro conversational remark about the weather - 'bit chilly around the early doors!'.

Effects Simulations of audio and visual phenomena, both natural and super-natural. Effects should be so well integrated with all the other aspects of the production that the audience will accept them as real. However, on thinking back the after the performance, the audience should be surprised that such events are possible in a theatre and wonder 'How did they do that!' Effects are sometimes called "Special Effects".

Electrics (1) All the lighting and other electrical equipment. (2) The technicians responsible for handling this equipment. Often shortened to LX.

Encore A response to applause by repeating all or part of a musical number. At the end of a concert, an encore may take the form of an extra item, usually chosen for its brevity and technical virtuosity.

End of the Pier In the heyday of summer shows in theatres on seaside piers, there were wide variations in standards. Although there were many exquisite theatre buildings presenting quality performances, it is the bottom end of the spectrum that is reflected in this phrase.

End Stage Theatre format where a single block of audience face a stage which extends from wall to wall without any framing by a proscenium.

Engagement Contract for a season of specified length or for the 'run of the show'.

ENSA Acronym for 'Entertainment National Service Association'. Also dubbed 'Every Night Something Awful', allegedly by the troops although the origin is more likely to have been a comedian's joke. From 1939 until 1945,

ENSA toured professional productions of every possible kind to entertain fighting troops in every war zone.

Ensemble A group who, by working together in many productions over an extended period, have developed a sensitive unity in their performance style.

Enter Actor coming into audience view by arriving on the acting area of the stage.

Entertainer An actor whose technical skills include singing, dancing, telling jokes, and generally engaging the audience by addressing them directly as if they were all personal friends.

Entertainment A performance which, at least superficially, is intended to make the audience feel good by providing pleasure rather than intellectual stimulation. However, even the most frothy light hearted entertainment is likely to trigger some deeper thoughts or emotions and this is acknowledged in the words above the proscenium of the Royal Theatre in Copenhagen - Ei Blot Tyl Lyst - which means Not for Entertainmenmt Only. Indeed, it is fundamental to the nature of theatre that entertainment is used as a vehicle for the propagation of profound ideas and exploration of human relationships.

Entr'Acte Music played between scenes, particularly when the audience return to their seats after an interval.

Entrance Any opening in the scenery where an actor gains access to the acting area and appears to the audience. In older theatres, the spaces between wings were called First Entrance, Second Entrance, Third Entrance, etc.

Entrance Cue A line of dialogue, situation or sound which signals to an actor that this is their moment to appear.

Entrance Music A few bars of music to accompany the entrance of a variety artiste. The tradition continues in pantomime where today's stars make their first entrance to the signature tune of the television series that has elevated them to stardom.

Epic (1) A performance on a broad sweep, deploying large resources, usually on a historic theme. (2) Drama concerned with social documentation or propaganda, presented in a non-naturalistic production style in order to engage the audiences' intellect rather than their emotion. Particularly associated with Bertholt Brecht.

Epilogue A short afterpiece to a play, tying up loose ends and perhaps commenting on moral issues which have been raised. The counterpart to a prologue at the beginning of a play. Both are older devices, not currently in stage use but not uncommon on television. Perhaps worthy of revival in an age when dramatic texts are not always models of clarity.

Episodic A type of dramatic construction where the action is not continuous but is a sequence of short self-contained scenes, each based on an incident in the story.

Equity Abbreviated name for the acting trade unions in the UK and US. British Equity is also a union for directors, designers and stage managers.

Establish Make clear to the audience who the character is that the actor is playing. In light entertainment, establishing is extended to developing a one-to-one rapport with the audience.

Exeunt An exit by more than one actor - especially by a crowd or chorus.

Exit An actor departing from the acting area and thus from audience view.

Exit Line Words spoken by an actor immediately before leaving the stage. Often significant for the plot and, in comedy, triggering a laughter response.

Experimental Departing from established writing, acting and production techniques in an effort to develop the art of the theatre.

Exposition The early sequences of a dramatic work where the basic structure of such matters as storyline, philosophy, background, characters, certainties and uncertainties, etc., is established.

Expressionism A production style where the acting, costumes, scenery and lighting are exaggerated and formalised, even distorted, to emphasise the inner significance of a play.

Extemporise Develop words and actions during a performance in response to the stimuli of the moment including the audience reaction.

Exterior Scenery representing an outdoor environment rather than an indoor (interior) one.

Extras Non-speaking actors, particularly those who swell a crowd scene.

Extravaganza A production using lavish resources to spectacular effect.

Factory Theatre people sometimes refer to their place of work as the factory or fun factory.

Fake Making something appear to happen without it actually doing so.

Fall of the Curtain The end of a performance.

False Proscenium A temporary inner proscenium designed to form an appropriate frame for a particular production. It is normally a little narrower and lower than the theatre's structural proscenium and positioned a very short distance upstage of it.

Family Circle A label occasionally used for a theatre balcony, usually as an alternative to upper circle or gallery.

Fan An auditorium format with curving seat rows which increase in length with their distance from the stage.

Fan Dancer A female dancer who uses large fans with considerable skill to obscure the nakedness or near nakedness of her body.

Farce A play where the humour is extracted from situations and coincidences which are exagerrated beyond the threshold of probability. Performances of farce require a high degree of credibilty in the acting and a slick pace to ensure that the audience do not have time to analyse the absurdities.

Farewell Last performance or tour of a performer's career.

Fat Part A role which is not only long but full of opportunity for displaying acting talent.

Feature Billing which is not so prominent as that accorded to a star, but still indicative of an important actor playing a key role.

Feed (1) Delivering lines to trigger replies which produce a laughter response from the audience. (2) An actor who speaks these feed lines. See **Foil, Straight Man.**

Feel Respond to the text, music and audience in a way which is instinctive rather than logical.

Female Impersonator A male actor who plays a female role, aiming for total reality. See **Dame** and **Drag**.

Festoon Curtain Curtain hung in decorative folds. See **Contour Curtain.**

Final Curtain The fall of the house curtain to mark the end of the play. Since 'final curtain' provides such a strong metaphor, its use is often extended to any life situation which marks a positive ending - including death.

Finale The last scene of a performance, particularly a musical.

First Call A variation of the percentage system in touring contracts when the visiting company does not receive a guaranteed minimum share but is entitled to (i.e. has first call on) the actual box office receipts up to a stipulated maximum.

Fire Curtain Steel shutter lowered to close the proscenium opening in the event of a backstage fire, isolating the flames and smoke to delay their spread in order to gain time for the audience to escape.

First Night The official opening performance to which the press are invited. However, this is rarely the first public performance because it will normally have been preceeded by one or more previews.

Fit Up (1) The initial assembly on the stage of the scenery and lights for a production. (2) An older name for a barnstorming theatre company who could adapt to playing in halls and improvised theatres of all types.

Five and Nine Pale and dark sticks of Leichner greasepaint which, in various proportions, traditionally provided the base make-up flesh-tone shade for an actor's face. Today's actors are more likely to select a suitable shade of water-based pancake foundation.

Five Minutes Please! A call given to the cast by the stage manager ten minutes before the advertised starting time of the performance to warn that there is only a further five minutes before actors who begin the first scene will be called to the stage.

Flashback Time shift to an earlier episode in the sequence of events covered by the play.

Flashbox Device for the electrical detonation of the pyrotechnic flash which traditionally accomompanies the entrance of immortals (baddies and fairies) in christmas pantomime.

Flats Lightweight timber frames covered with scenic canvas. Now usually covered with plywood and consequently no longer light in weight.

Fleshings Tights, or a complete body stocking, in a skin shade.

Flier Publicity leaflet, usually no larger than A5, produced in large quantities and particularly intended for casual pick-up by potential ticket buyers. See **Throwaway.**

Floats Footlights - from the time when the light came from wicks floating in an oil reservoir.

Flop Production which fails to attract any significant size of audience.

Fluff Make mistakes with the text.

Flys The area above the stage into which scenery can be hoisted out of sight of the audience.

FOH (Front of House) Everything on the audience side of the proscenium.

Foil (1) Fencing weapon. (2) Actor who works with a comedian, feeding lines and being the victim of the comedian's jokes. See **Feed, Straight Man, Stooge.**

Fold Premature end to the anticipated run of a production.

Follies Revue which features particularly lavish staging and costumes.

Follow Spot Spotlight with which an operator follows an actor around the stage. In addition to providing illumination, a hard-edged circle of light is often regarded as a mark of star status. See **Limelight.**

Footlights A row of lights along the front of the stage, once a major source of illumination for the actor's face but now used only for a special effect due to the unnatural angle of the light and the wish to minimise any barrier between actor and audience. See **Floats.**

Forestage The area in front of the house curtain on a proscenium stage.

Foundation The basic make-up tint applied to the face.

Found Space A venue which was not designed as a theatre building but has been adapted to house performances.

Fourth Wall The invisible wall through which the audience see a play in a box set.

Four Walls A theatre rental agreement providing minimum facilities and equipment. Usually involves a fixed payment rather than a box-office percentage.

Foyer Audience area other than the auditorium, particularly the area immediately inside the entrance doors from the street.

Freeze Cessation of all movement by the actors, occasionally for dramatic effect, but more usually during prolonged audience laughter.

Friends Organisation of regular theatregoers who support and fundraise for a particular theatre.

Fringe An alternative name for **Alternative Theatre.** The name originates from Edinburgh which is renowned for the ever increasing number of alternative performances on the fringe of the more formal International Festival.

Frocks Stage clothes worn by actors, both male and female.

From the Front The stage as viewed by the audience.

Front All parts of a theatre which are not backstage. See **Out Front.**

Frontcloth (1) Painted scenic cloth hanging at the front of the stage. (2) Variety act who can perform in the shallow depth of stage in front of such a cloth.

Front of House (FOH) All areas of a theatre on the audience side of the proscenium.

Front Row The row of seating nearest the stage.

Full Stage A scene using all the available stage depth.

Full Up A very bright state of stage lighting.

FUF Full Up Finish. Encouraging applause by an increase in light brightness over the final bars of a musical number.

Funding Financial support, usually from a mix of national government, local government and sponsors, to cover the gap between operating costs and trading income from ticket and ancilliary sales.

G

Gaff Older, mostly 19th century, word for a downmarket theatre, possibly with only improvised facilities, presenting robust performances at cheap prices to an audience with an uninhibited response. Also known as **Penny gaff.**

Gag (1) Comedy sequence culminating in a big laugh, known as the tag, which is often followed by an exit or a blackout. (2) Make exaggerated facial expressions.

Gallery Topmost balcony, so high that it is often known as **The Gods.**

Garden, The The Royal Opera House in London's Covent Garden.

General Abbreviation of **General Rehearsal** which is the opera house name for the final dress rehearsal.

George Spelvin (1) Name used on programmes and posters printed before a role has been cast (US). (2) Name used when an actor is playing two parts. UK equivalent is Walter Plinge.

Gesture Movement of a hand or an arm to make a dramatic point.

Get Across Succeed in projecting a character or an idea to the audience.

Get In (1) Unloading a production into a theatre. Also known as 'load in' and 'bump in' in various parts of the world. (2) The door through which scenery enters and leaves the theatre.

Get Out (1) Dismantling a production and loading it into transport for removal from the theatre. Also known as 'load out', 'bump out', and even 'chuckout', in various parts of the world. (2) The minimum weekly box office receipts that will cover the production expenses to the point of break even.

Get the Bird When the audience show obvious, and probably audible, disapproval of performing skills.

Get the Hook When solo performers are signalled from the wings to terminate their act and leave the stage, particularly if they have overrun their alloted time or are perhaps just failing to entertain the audience. There is a lost tradition that performers failing to take the hint were fished off with a hook on a long pole. Given the distance from wings to centre stage, the effect must have been psychological rather than physical.

Ghost Glide See **Corsican Trap.**

Ghost Walks, The Sometimes 'The Ghost Walks on Fridays'. The paying out of weekly salaries. More formally known as **Treasury.**

Gig An engagement to take part in a performance.

Glitter (1) Minute particles of reflective material added to scenery and costumes to make them sparkle. (2) The production style arising from such treatment.

Go (1) The action word to instigate any change of scenery, light, sound or special effect. (2) A measure of success as in 'How did it go?'

Go Behind Go backstage from the front-of-house.

Gods The highest gallery in a theatre, close to the ceiling.

Go Off Make an exit from the acting area.

Go On For . . . Perform as understudy to . . .

Go Up The beginning of the performance, whether or not there is an actual curtain to go up. See **Come Down.**

Going Up Warning spoken by a stage manager immediately prior to cueing the rise of a house curtain.

Going Round Visiting the actors in their dressing rooms immediately after a performance.

Good House An audience which fills most of the seats and responds well to the performance.

Grand Circle The lowest balcony. An alternative for **Dress Circle**, particularly in an age when audience no longer wear evening dress.

Grand Guignol A short play depicting horrors such as murder, rape and mutilation in a sensational manner intended to thrill rather than shock.

Greasepaint Traditional make-up of pigmented grease solidified into stick form.

Great White Way New York's Broadway and its theatres.

Green The part of the stage visible to the audience. There are many theories as to the origin, varying from the green baize stage carpet formerly used for tragedy to the cockney rhyming slang of 'stage' with 'greengage'.

Green Room Room adjacent to the stage (i.e. the 'green') for the actors to meet and relax.

Gross The total amount of money taken at the theatre box office - normally in one week.

Groundlings Audience who stood at floor level to look up at the stage in an Elizabethan theatre. (Seated audience looked down from galleries).

Groupies Sycophantic fans who are so obsessed with particular performers that they follow them around tour venues.

Gypsy A performer, particularly in musical theatre.

H

Half, The A call given to the actors half an hour before they will be called to the stage for the beginning of the performance. The Half is normally called 35 minutes before the advertised time of commencement (Subsequent calls are 'the quarter', 'five minutes' and 'beginners').

Halls, The Musical Halls and the Variety Theatres into which they developed.

Hallkeeper The traditional title for the person responsible for stage door security. Often called **Stage Door Keeper**, although the word 'security' is increasingly featured in the job title.

Ham An actor giving a performance lacking in subtlety of voice, gesture and interpretation. Suggested sources of the name include 'hamateur' and the ostentatiously decorated "Ham House" in Richmond. But it is probably a contraction of 'Hamfatter', a name for barnstorming actors who used ham fat to remove make-up.

Hand Applause.

Happening A performance event rooted in improvisation and involving various media. Tends to be physically rather than textually based.

Harlequinade A sequence, popular in Victorian Christmas pantomime, featuring the characters of the commedia dell arte.

Heavy (1) A serious role requiring a dramatically exaggerated performance. (2) An actor who plays such parts.

High Camp A particularly exaggerated form of **Camp**.

High Comedy Plays where the laughter is a response to thought-provoking dialogue between witty articulate characters.

Histrionics Acting, particularly in an exaggerated style.

Hit A very successful script, production or individual performance.

Hold Keep the attention of an audience.

Hoofer A dancer, particularly in musicals.

Hook See **Get the Hook**.

Horseshoe Shape of the balcony curves in a traditional Italianate theatre auditorium.

Hot Ticket A very successful show for which tickets are in heavy demand.

House The auditorium and the audience.

House Curtain see **House Tabs**

House Full Board placed outside a theatre to inform (and boast!) that all seats have been sold.

Housekeeper Supervisor of a theatre's cleaning staff.

Houselights The decorative lighting in the auditorium.

House Manager The management team member responsible for supervising all parts of the theatre accessible to the public, welcoming the audience and ensuring their comfort. Good house management ensures that an audience approaches the performance in a receptive mood, enjoys their evening and departs with a desire to return in future.

House Seats Seats held back by the box office for possible use by important or influential visitors. They are released for sale shortly before the performance if it becomes apparent that they will not be required for this purpose.

House Tabs The main curtain filling the proscenium opening. Usually made from a rich velour fabric. By long tradition, the most common colour scheme is red with gold trimming.

Hurry Music An accompaniment played as an underscoring to action and dialogue as support for an impression of haste.

I

IATSE International Alliance of Theatrical Stage Employees and Motion Picture Operatives. US trade union for stage technicians.

Impresario A producer. Usually reserved for one who operates with a considerable degree of individuality and flamboyance.

Improvisation Unscripted dialogue and movement developed during rehearsal or performance. Improvisation in the rehearsal room may be used as one of the methods by which a group of actors and their director work with, or without, a writer to devise a play. It may also be used as a rehearsal exercise technique to help actors probe hidden depths in the play or discover aspects of their roles. While a few production styles include improvisation, most perfomance use is related to a cover up when something goes wrong.

In (1) Scenery stored in the flys above the stage is lowered 'in' and raised 'out' rather than 'up' and 'down'. (2) A production is said to be 'in rehearsal' or 'in performance'. (3) Contraction of **In Front.**

Incidental Music Music selected or specially composed to integrate with the action of a play.

In Front An important visitor watching the performance from the auditorium is said to be 'in front'. (Whereas someone closely connected with the production and watching the performance would be said to be **Out Front**)

In Town In London.

Ingenue (1) A young female role to which such adjectives as innocent, attractive, sweet, naive and young may be applied. (2) An actress specialising in portrayal of such roles.

In One A scene played at the front of the stage.

In the Round Staging format where the acting area is surrounded by audience seating. Rarely round, usually rectangular or polygonal.

Intellectual Property The ownershp rights in a product resulting from creative decsions. This tends to be less tangible than the products of other areas of manufacture and include scripts, scores, productions, designs, etc. See **Copyright, Royalties.**

Interior An indoor scene.

Intermission An interval.

Interval A pause when the houselights are on and the audience may leave the auditorium if they wish.

Iron The fire retardant safety curtain separating the stage from the auditorium.

It Will Be All Right On The Night The traditional optimistic response to rehearsal problems.

J

Joey A clown. Derived from the great English clown, Joseph Grimaldi.

Jump Forgetting, or intentionally eliminating, sections of dialogue.

Juvenile Good looking young actor or actress, usually in early twenties, playing a romantic role of the same age.

K

Kabuki A traditional form of Japanese popular theatre combining drama, music and mime. There is considerable emphasis on spectacle and all parts are played by men.

Kill (1) To remove a prop or item of scenery. An item which has been killed becomes **Dead**. Sometimes used as an alternative to **Strike**, particularly if a piece of scenery is to be removed permanently from the production. (2) Extinguish a light.

Kill a Laugh Distractions or poor timing which prevent the audience appreciating the full humour of a comedy line or situation.

Kill a Line Diminishing the impact of dialogue by poor timing or by a distraction. Usually caused by an actor other than the one speaking the killed lines.

Kitchen Sink Plays involving the day-to-day living problems of ordinary people and consequently tending to be set around a kitchen table rather than in an elegant drawing room.

Knockabout Comedy where the laughs are based on physical interaction, usually involving misfortune.

L

Lane, The The Theatre Royal in London's Drury Lane.

Laugh Line A sentence in a script which produces a laughter response from the audience.

Last Night The final performance of a production.

Lead The principal role in a play.

Left Actor's left, facing the audience. See **P.S.**

Leg Vertical strip of fabric used mainly for masking, cither decorative or neutral.

Legit Legitimate. The dramatic theatre and its actors, excluding all other types of performance and performer, particularly singers and dancers.

Leg Show A dance production which emphasises female glamour with the aid of abbreviated costumes.

Leichner Make-up manufacturer whose name has become synonymous with greasepaint sold in stick form. Generations of performers achieved their desired skin tone for any role by a carefully judged combination of Leichener sticks numbers five and nine.

Libraries Ticket agencies, especially in London, who have an allocation of seats for which they charge a booking fee to the customer in addition to obtaining a commission from the theatre.

Libretto The words of an opera.

Licence Formal authorisation document which details the conditions under which a theatre may be opened to the public or a play may be performed. Licences to operate theatres are primarily concerned with safety matters while, following the abolition of formal censorship in many parts of the world, licenses to perform now relate mainly to copyright.

Lifts (1) Elevations of ballerinas by their male partners. (2) Sections of the stage floor which are mechanised to rise and fall. (3) Shoes with extra thick soles and heels to increase an actor's height.

Light Comedian A performer who endeavours to amuse an audience by means of good-humoured wit, perhaps accompanied by a little song and dance.

Light Comedy Good-humoured play which seeks to amuse with very little attempt to explore situations, characters or emotions in any depth.

Limelight A block of lime, made brilliantly incandescent by the flame from a mixture of oxygen and hydrogen, introduced intensely powerful light beams into the Victorian theatre. Both the spotlights and their operators became known as **Limes**, a term still used in today's followspotting.

Lines (1) The words of a play's dialogue. (2) The wires or ropes on which scenery and lights are suspended.

Line rehearsal A rehearsal which concentrates on the words, particularly the accurate memorising of the text.

Literary Manager See **Dramaturgy.**

Little Theatre An amateur theatre, particularly one with a strong committment to the community in which it is located.

Live A production which is performed afresh for each audience rather than reproduced from a recording on film or tape.

Living Newspaper A revue based on dramatisation of current social and political events, tending to present the material in the brash, often polemical, style of media reporting.

Load In/Out See **Get In/Out.**

Lobby The entrance foyer (particularly in US).

Long Run A successful production which is scheduled to remain in a theatre for as long as it continues to draw a nightly audience. This often involves one or more changes of cast. See **Mousetrap, Whodunnit.**

Lord Chamberlain The government department formerly responsible for licensing plays, prior to the abolition of censorship in the UK.

Low Comedy Humour derived from behaviour which tends towards the obvious, vulgar and physical rather than the elegant and witty.

Luvvie A theatre professional with a gushing manner and a tendency to address everyone as 'Darling!'

LX Contraction for electrics, both the equipment and the technicians.

Lyrics The words of a song in a musical or of an aria in an opera.

Lyric Theatre Musical theatre, particularly opera and ballet.

M

Machines Stage equipment, especially that used in the 18th century and earlier, to produce spectacular visual effects.

Maitre De Ballet Ballet master with particular responsibilities for maintainimg standards through daily 'class' practice.

Mainstage Productions in a principal auditorium rather than in an associated studio. Consequently any reference to a 'mainstage production' implies (possibly) some degree of orthodoxy and (probably) that any minimalism is the result of artistic policy rather than resource shortage.

Make An Entrance Come on to the stage in such a manner as to immediately become the focus of attention.

Make It Achieve and sustain a successful career.

Make-Up (1) Emphasising facial structure to enable reactions to be projected across the considerable distances involved in a large auditorium. The emphasis may be selective in order to stress characteristics appropriate to the role; this may involve considerable restructuring of the face when it is necessary to indicate ageing or illness. When appropriate, make-up may be applied to other exposed body surfaces. (2) The cosmetic and prosthetic material applied in the course of effecting these facial or body changes.

Marquee The street frontage of a theatre, particularly the canopy over the pavement, on which the title of the show and its stars are displayed in lights.

Marie Tempest Door closing device named after the famous actress.

Mark Speak the lines and make the moves without entering the character or projecting a performance. A way for an actor to save creative energy during a long technical rehearsal.

Maroon Electrically fired pyrotechnic which provides the sound effect of an exploding bomb.

Masking Neutral or decorative scenery which defines the acting area and conceals the technical areas of the stage.

Masque Spectacular renaissance entertainment, usually presented on a specially constructed stage as part of a celebration. There was often little or no dialogue; emphasis was placed on music, songs, dance, mime and elaborate costumes.

Matcham Frank Matcham (1854-1920) was the most prolific and renowned architect of Britain's 19th century commercial theatre building boom. Adept at utilising small irregularly shaped sites to maximum effect, he was skilled in designing the richly decorative auditorium which a popular theatre needed to offer as an escape from the social conditions of rapid industrialisation.

Material The script and business of a comedian's act.

Matinee A morning or, more commonly, an afternoon performance.

Matinee Idol Young male actor, with a particularly starry appeal to the ladies, in the days when afternoon tea trays were served to stalls and dress circle patrons at their seats during intervals in West End matinees.

Matter The words to be printed on a poster or programme.

Matured The advance box-office sales for today's performance.

Melodrama (1) A play with musical accompaniment to spoken dialogue. (2) A play where the contrast between virtue and villainy is exaggerated in a sensationally implausible plot which always ends in the triumph of virtue.

Method An acting technique developed from Stanislavski ideas by Lee Strasberg at the Actors' Studio in New York. Its reliance on inner motivation can lead to a style of acting where introspection tends to inhibit projection of both voice and character. Consequently it has perhaps been more successful on film than on stage.

Mezzanine (1) US for the lowest balcony (Grand or Dress Circle in UK) (2) Area used for handling traps and elevators immediately under the stage (US).

Miked Actors voices reinforced by personal wireless microphones. Normally used in musicals rather than in spoken drama.

Milk Squeezing the maximum applause from an audience, particularly by risking an extra curtain call when the applause is dying away.

Mime Conveying character and plot by using only gesture without help from spoken or sung text.

Minor Theatre Originally an 18th or early 19th century British theatre without a license to perform drama and consequently forced to get around the law by various devices, particularly the inclusion of songs and musical underscoring. See **Melodrama, Patent Theatres.**

Minimalism Reduction of the stage environment to only the most significant and essential elements. Ideally, a production style rather than a response to insufficient resources.

Minstrels White actors blacked-up to perform the music of the old American deep south.

Miracle Play Drama based on biblical events, mainly those associated with miraculous events in the lives of saints.

Miscast Actors given roles for which they lack the right kind of talent and/or physical appearance to enable them to give a satisfactory interpretation.

Mise En Scene The total environment in which a play is realised - the sets, costumes, lights, sound, effects, props, movement etc - and the way in which the actors interact with this environment.

Mixed Notices Critical reviews which, in varying degree, tend to hover around suggestions of mediocrity but none of which are particularly positive in either dismissing a performance or enthusing about it.

Modern Dress Period play performed in today's costume.

Morality Medieval allegorical play where the characters represent abstract vices and virtues.

Motivation Plausible reasons for a character's response to a particular situation.

Motley Multicoloured patch-work costumes originating with Harlequin of the commedia dell' arte. Now given a wider meaning which embraces the assumption of an acting role, encapsulated in the aria from I Palgiacci 'On with the Motley, the paint and the powder . . .'

Mount Prepare and perform a production.

Mousetrap The longest running **Whodunnit.**

Moves The positions on the stage taken by the actors during the progress of a performance.

Moving the Line (Rope) Altering the row at which seat prices change in response to fluctuations in the demand for tickets.

Mug Act with facial expressions exaggerated to the point of caricature.

Mummers Originally the actors in British medieval plays about folk heroes, especially St George. Sometimes now used as a label for actors generally.

Mummerset A generalised regional dialect adopted by actors in plays set in unidentified regions of the English countryside.

Municipal Theatre A theatre directly funded and managed by a civic authority.

Musical A theatre form where the action is carried forward in songs and dances.

Musical Comedy Lightweight entertainment where the musical numbers are an additional commentary rather than an integral part of the storyline.

Musical Director Often abbreviated to M.D. The member of the production team responsible for rehearsing vocal and instrumental music and maintaining performance standards. Usually conducts at least the initial performances.

Music Cue (1) An entrance, speech, scene change, light change or effect which is signalled by a music note or phrase. (2) A verbal or visual event which is the signal for music to begin.

Music Hall (1) Late 19th and early 20th century popular entertainment comprising a series of self-contained acts. Originally presented to an audience at refreshment tables but popularity soon led to the adoption of the higher density of conventional theatre seating. (2) Theatres dedicated to the Music

Hall performance format.

Musician's Union The trade union representing the orchestral musicians in theatres. Their negotiations have not been confined to fees and working conditions but have strived to ensure that theatre performances retain their live quality by using pit musicians rather than recordings.

Music Theatre With increasing interaction between theatre forms, the traditional labels of opera, operetta, musical comedy and musical have become increasingly meaningless. The term 'Music Theatre' embraces all forms of staged performance where singing, dancing and music (whether traditionally played or digitally generated) make a more significant contribution than the spoken word.

Mysteries Medieval plays on a biblical theme, particularly one dealing with the life of Christ. In their most developed form, they became a cycle that covered events from the creation to the last judgement.

N

Name An actor who is sufficiently well known to be regarded as a positive asset in promoting ticket sales.

Narrator An actor, speaking directly to the audience, who tells a story which links a sequence of scenes.

National, The The Royal National Theatre on London's South Bank.

National Company A performing ensemble funded by the central government of a country and regarded as a cultural flagship of that country.

National Theatre A producing theatre located in a capital city with a particular remit to safeguard and develop national dramatic traditions within an international context. See **Royal National Theatre.**

Nativity A play about events surrounding the birth of Jesus Christ in Bethlehem.

NATTKE National Association of Theatrical, Television and Kine Employees. Former union for stage crew and front of house staff. Now subsumed within **BECTU.**

Naturalism A production style which seeks to minimise the small exaggerations of normal behaviour which are necessary to project the fine detail of a character to an audience in the artificial environment of a theatre. Naturalistic acting does not necessarily require a realistic stage environment: minimal selective scenery can offer effective support.

Night Club Late night venue with musical entertainment performed to an audience seated at tables where refreshments are served.

Noh Theatre Traditional classic drama theatre of Japan with a highly formalised production style where masked actors perform in a special type of theatre building.

Noises Off Sound effects relating to a happening offstage, i.e. outside the stage environment which is visible to the audience.

Non-Commercial Strictly speaking, a theatre organisation which is not constituted to distribute profits to shareholders. However, the label tends to be applied to any production which is directed towards a minority audience.

No Play: No Pay A phrase used in old contracts - the author was engaged on such a contract as recently as 1956. When no theatre was available, it enabled touring managements to suspend the tour for a week (a 'week out') without paying the company. It also provided a powerful incentive towards meeting that oldest of theatre clichés - the show must go on.

Nose Putty Plastic substance used to alter the shape of an actor's nose when making up.

Not A Dry Eye In The House The summit of success for tragedy.

Not A Dry Seat In The House A somewhat indelicate expression of success for comedy. See **Rolling in the Aisles.**

Notes Comments made by the director to actors and production team after a non-stopping rehearsal.

Notice (1) A press review of a production. (2) The announcement posted on the callboard giving the date of the end of a production's run and formally terminating all 'run-of-the-play' contracts with effect from that date.

Number A musical item, particularly a song.

Number One (Two/Three) Until early in the second half of the twentieth century, touring shows and touring theatres were informally graded on the basis of location and facilities. The grandeur of a theatre was reflected in the price of its seats and consequently its ability to meet the cost of star names.

N.T. Britain's Royal National Theatre on the London's South Bank.

O

Off An actor who misses an entrance.

Off Broadway Secondary level of New York theatres where productions require a lower level of financial investment than on Broadway. This is a consequence of several factors, particularly more relaxed union agreements.

Off Off Broadway Escalating Off Broadway costs have resulted in another tier of even smaller theatres where plays can be given try out productions without excessive financial risk.

Offer A firm proposal of engagement setting out basic details such as dates and fees but subject to the signing of a formal contractual agreement.

Offstage The masked areas to the sides and rear of the acting area.

Old Pro An experienced actor who can be depended upon to behave with impeccable professionalism. Old Pros pride themselves in taking all problems in their stride.

Olio (Oleo) Traditional US name for a painted cloth hanging downstage, flown by rolling, and used for playing a scene or vaudeville act while the next scene was being set behind. The scene in front was often known as an Olio Act or Olio Scene. Similar to UK usage of **Frontcloth.**

Oliviers Annual awards, under the auspices of the Society of London Theatre, for excellence in London west end productions and national theatre companies.

On Visible to the audience.

On/Off Movement towards the centre or towards the side of the stage

One Acter Short play without interval.

One Liner Free standing concise witty remark.

One Man Show A complete evening's entertainment performed by a single actor.

One Night Stand A show which gives only a single performance in each venue.

Onstage The acting area visible to the audience.

On Stage, Please A call to actors or crew to come to the stage area.

On The Book The member of the stage management team (Deputy Stage Manager in the UK) responsible for recording actor moves in the prompt book during rehearsals, then calling the cues during performances. Also prompts if necessary.

On The Road An actor or production which is currently playing in a sequence of venues across the country (particularly US).

On Tour An actor or production which is playing in a sequence of venues across the country (particularly UK).

O.P. 'Opposite prompt' side of the stage - i.e. stage right (actor's right when facing the audience). See P.S.

Open (1) A production which is currently giving performances. (2) Seats which are unsold.

Open Air Theatre A performance venue where stage and auditorium are totally or partly unprotected from the weather.

Open Call An audition where any actor can offer themselves for casting without invitation.

Open Cold Commence a run of performances in an important theatre, particularly on Broadway or in the West End, without a prior tour and possibly even without a series of previews.

Opening The first performance.

Opera Theatre form where all the words are sung rather than spoken.

Opera Bouffe Form of opera where the plot is treated in a light hearted manner and set to frothy accessible music.

Opera Glasses Small binnoculars enabling audience to have a closer view of actors faces. Older theatres often had (and a few have retained) opera glasses located in seat-back fittings for coin rental.

Opera House A rather grand theatre with lavish technical facilities, richly decorated auditorium, and impressive foyers. The term does not necessarily imply the performance of opera.

Operetta A form of opera where the plot is not too serious, the music is melodic, and much of the dialogue is likely to be spoken rather than sung.

Opposite A pair of leading actors, usually male and female, with roles of nearly equal importance are said to be playing 'opposite' each other.

Option An agreement with a playwright giving the holder the exclusive right to produce a play within a stipulated period of time.

Orchestra US term for the audience seating at auditorium floor level. (**Stalls** in UK).

Orchestra Pit Space for musicians in front of the stage. Formerly at auditorium floor level where it still needs to be for proper acoustic balance when performing older operas with original instruments. Now sunken and with the rear part located underneath the stage.

Orchestra Stalls Formerly the seats nearest to the stage at auditorium floor level. They were comfortably upholstered in contrast to the simpler chairs or even hard benches of the rear seating area known as the **Pit**. Today the term refers to the entire seating at ground floor level and 'orchestra' has been largely dropped to leave simply **Stalls**.

Original Cast The actors who gave the first interpretation of the roles.

OTT Over The Top. A performance which is exaggerated to the point of being barely credible, particularly in relation to the performances by the other actors in the production. However, OTT carries an implication that the actor's performance was enjoyed by the person who labelled it thus.

Out Front The auditorium. As in 'the author is out front tonight' and 'Play this scene out front' meaning that the scene should be projected directly to the audience'.

Out of Town A performance away from London or New York, particularly the opening of a show which is intended to play in these cities in due course.

Overact Performing in an exaggerated manner.

Over Parted An actor cast in a role for which their experience and/or talent is insufficient to enable them to give a satisfactory performance.

Overture Music played prior to the commencement of a performance. Overtures were originally intended to be played with the house curtain down, but today's directors tend to devise silent movement to accompany the music.

Overture and Beginners Call given to inform everyone backstage that, as the performance will commence in five minutes, the orchestra should now go into the pit and the actors in the opening scene should come to the stage. The wording dates from the era of Call Boys. With today's microphones, the stage manager is more likely to give separate beginner's calls to the orchestra and to individual members of the cast.

P

Pace Not so much the speed as the tempo at which a scene is performed. An apparently steady pace usually conceals subtle variations, with both the overall speed and the variations within it influenced by audience response.

Pad Add text, music or business which extends the length of a scene without improving its structure or purpose.

Pageant Large scale re-enactment of a historic occasion, usually in the open air, often on the site where the commemorated event originally took place and involving many citizens, bands of musicians and probably horses from the local community.

Pancake Water-soluble make-up in solid form. Applied with a sponge, it has largely replaced traditional sticks of greasepaint, particularly for foundation purposes.

Pantomime The use of movement and gesture to convey character and plot. See **Christmas Pantomime, Commedia Dell' Arte, Harlequinade.**

Paper Complimentary tickets.

Papering (The House) Using complimentary tickets to disguise a poor response at the box office.

Paper Theatres Model stages and scenery printed in colour. Often called Toy Theatres and used as such, although they are also a serious resource for the history of scenery, costumes and proscenium architecture.

Parody Dialogue or acting which extracts humour from a situation or person by using imitation to ridicule.

Part A role in a play.

Pass Door Door near the proscenium, leading directly from backstage to the front-of-house. Usually narrow and made of steel because it is a break in the fire wall intended to retard the spread of any stage fire to the auditorium.

Custom restricts passage through this door during performance to a very small number of essential users.

Passerelle Walkway between orchestra pit and audience for showgirls to promenade.

Passion The major ingredient for performance (as in the phrase 'all you need is planks and a passion').

Passion Play Drama about the events surrounding the crucifixion of Jesus Christ.

Pastiche Show constructed from a patchwork of items selected from several different dramatic texts or music scores. The selection may be from a single or several writers/composers.

Pastoral Play or opera idolising rustic life.

Patent Theatres From 1662 until 1842, letters patent granted by Charles II gave privileges to Covent Garden and Drury Lane Theatres which virtually placed them in a monopoly position for the presentation of Drama. Opera and other entertainments involving music were not regarded as drama and this led to a gradual erosion of the monopoly. See **Minor Theatres.**

Patron General name for a member of an audience, although sometimes used for a category of supporter who donates a prescribed minimum annual sum.

Patter The spoken parts of a variety act.

Peephole A tiny aperture, usually a hole in the house curtain, through which it is possible to observe the audience from the stage. In Georgian theatres, peepholes were located in the proscenium doors.

Pencilled An unconfirmed booking. Often moves to 'heavy pencil' before confirmation by contract.

Penny Gaff See **Gaff**.

Penny Plain, Twopence Coloured Prints of line drawings of Victorian actors were sold for a penny. Hand coloured versions were two pence.

People's Theatre Early 20th century idealism sought a community playhouse which would address, in an entertaining way, the issues concerning all sections of a community.

Percentage Many of the contractual arrangements in the theatre industry include a percentage element. Division of box office receipts between a touring production and its host theatre was traditionally on a percentage basis with 65% to the touring company being common. This has now become 70%, 75% or even higher. Many of today's contracts include a guaranteed element within the percentage or involve a 'first call' whereby the first block of box office receipts, up to a stipulated sum, accrue to the visiting company. Writers and production team royalties are percentage based and star actor's salaries are often related, through percentage, to their box-office attraction. Ten percent of salary is the traditional remuneration for agents, although some take a higher percentage when they undertake detailed career management services for their clients.

Perform Convey an idea or emotion to an audience through speech, music, and movement, with or without the support of a scenographic environment.

Performance An event intended to entertain and stimulate the minds and senses of an audience through the use of such media as acting, singing and dancing.

Performance Art A presentation, possibly accompanied by non-textual sounds, where the human performers(s) are an integral part of a visual environment which may include a wide range of media.

Period Presentation of a play in the settings, costumes and behaviour of a period earlier than today.

Perspective The proportions, painting and relationships of the elements in a scenic environment arranged to maximise the audience's impression of stage depth.

Photo Call A session when production and/or press photographs are taken. Formerly a separate call, now tends to be incorporated into a dress rehearsal.

Physical Theatre A performance style which places emphasis on acting with the body.

Pick Up Re-start an interrupted rehearsal from a convenient point (the 'pick up' point) for continuity.

Piece The work - i.e. play, opera, ballet, musical, etc - to be performed.

Pierrots Seaside entertainers who wore a characteristic uniform costume throughout the performance which was often given in the open air. Now, alas, extinct.

Pinteresque Dramatic writing in the style of Harold Pinter, characterised by oblique or inverted dialogue with communication, between actors and with the audience, tending to be focused on what remains unsaid during the frequent pauses.

Pit (1) Area in front of the stage for musicians. Originally at floor level but now usually sunk and often extending underneath the stage. (2) In the Georgian theatre, the pit was an audience seating area at ground floor level. In the Victorian theatre, the front of this area became the orchestra stalls and only the rear was designated as pit.

Places, Please Warning given by stage managers in the US that actors should take their opening positions on the stage as the curtain is about to rise.

Plan Box-office chart of the layout of the auditorium showing seats sold and those available for sale.

Plant (1) Introduction of an idea, object or character which will not become significant until later in the progression of the plot. (2) An actor placed among the audience so that the actor appears to be a member of the audience.

Play (1) As a noun, a dramatic work using speech as its principal medium. (2) As a verb, to perform a role in a dramatic performance.

Play as Cast A contractual term for agreement to perform all and any roles selected by the management.

Playbill A poster advertising a theatre performance, originally describing the production in such detail that it also served as a programme.

Play Doctor A writer-director who is called in to advise, assist and possibly take over a production which is getting a poor audience reception - usually during previews, or on tour prior to Broadway or the West End.

Played (Name of theatre or town) Performed in that theatre or town.

Player An actor.

Play for Laughs Acting in a way intended to extract the maximum humour from the dialogue and situations, even at the expense of perhaps imposing some superficiality on the interpretation.

Playgoer A member of the audience who attends performances regularly and has something of a passion for theatre.

Playhouse A theatre on a sufficiently intimate scale for housing productions based on speech.

Playing Performing.

Play It Straight Acting a script exactly as written, without attempting to place an interpretation on the words or to extract any hidden humour.

Playlet A drama piece which is shorter than a full evening's entertainment.

Play of Ideas Drama which focuses on an appeal to the audience's intellect rather than their emotions.

Play-On Music to accompany an entrance, particularly of variety acts or pantomime actors.

Play-Off Accompaniment to an exit or the end of a scene in a musical.

Play Opposite See **Opposite.**

Play Out Music to accompany the exit of the audience after the bows at the end of a performance.

Play Reading Performance of a script where the actors may have had some rehearsal but have not memorised the words. They may remain seated or make some simple movements.

Play's The Thing, The Hamlet quote annexed by theatre workers to justify their labours, and by drama critics to focus on the importance of the text.

Play To Capacity Have a full house.

Play to the Gallery Project a performance towards the most responsive section of the audience. This was traditionally the galleryites but the focus today is more likely to be receptive people scattered throughout all seating sections in the auditorium.

Play Within a Play (1) A brief play which takes place within the structure of another dramatic text. (2) A device sometimes used by directors who opt to produce a play as if it were being performed by a company of itinerant amateur or professional actors.

Playwright A dramatist, i.e. someone who makes plays (ie wrights by writing).

Plinge See **Walter Plinge.**

Plot (1) The events of a play rather than their meaning. (2) List of preparations and actions required during a performance.

Point Emphasise a line, movement, or gesture to stress its significance in the development of plot or character.

Pointe (1) A ballet dancer balancing, 'en pointe', on the tip of her toe. (2) The shoe with an inserted block which makes this balance possible.

Point of Command The position on the stage from which actors feel they can embrace the attention of all, or very nearly all, members of the audience. Usually located on the centre line of the stage but at a distance from the front edge, varying with the architecture of each particular theatre.

Poor Theatre The concept that theatre must be stripped of all illusionary devices such as scenery, costume, make-up, lighting other than illumination, and sounds other than those made by the actors themselves. The term was coined by Polish director Jerry Grotowski who believed that such devices, rather than provide support for the actor, formed a barrier between actor and audience.

Popular Prices A marketing slogan for lower than average seat costs.

Poster Large pictorial advert designed for placing in prominent sites to bring a production to the notice of a potential audience. From a distance, good posters present an image sufficiently dynamic to entice a theatregoer to cross the road for a closer look which will reveal clear information about place, time, cost and cast.

Post the Bond Deposit sufficient cash to pay salaries and fees in lieu of notice if the production suddenly fails. This is a US term for an action which is universal for commercial theatre in UK and much of the world.

Practical Anything which has to work rather than just look as if it could work.

Premier Danseur Leading male dancer in Ballet.

Premiere Danseuse Leading female dancer in Ballet.

Premiere The first performance, particularly of a newly written piece, although sometimes used for the first performance of a new production of an established work.

Presence An actor's ability to hold an audience, irrespective of the quality of the text or the production.

Press (1) Drama critics and show business feature writers. (2) Critical response to a production as in 'a good press'.

Preview A performance given prior to the formal first night. The audience understand and accept that the production is still being polished and are normally compensated for this by reduced prices.

Prima Donna Leading female singer in opera, often playing the title role.

Principals Actors cast in major roles. In musicals, all actors other than chorus.

Principal Boy The hero of a Christmas pantomime, traditionally played by an actress. In recent years there has been some tendency towards casting male actors, particularly pop stars. However, there are still many real principal boys to be seen each year.

Principal Girl The heroine of a Christmas pantomime who marries the principal boy in the final scene. In view of the gender complexities of panto-mime casting, it should perhaps be recorded that the principal girl is always played by an actress.

Pro Contraction for **Professional.** See **Old Pro, Real Pro.**

Produce The bringing together of actors, production team and the physical apparatus of the stage to prepare and perform an interpretation of a script and/or score.

Producer Formerly (and sometimes still in opera) the person who directs the actors. Now the packager who brings together script, theatre, production team, possibly the stars and certainly the money.

Product With the growth of formal marketing in theatres, performances tend to be regarded as manufactured goods and sold as a consumer product.

Production The process of realising a text, music score or scenario for performance by bringing together all necessary elements including performers, creative team, venue and funding.

Production Manager Responsible for technical preparation, including budgeting and scheduling, of new productions.

Production Number A musical sequence involving soloists and a large chorus, often with spectacular scenery. Although an integral segment of a complete work, each production number has an internal structure which is often sufficient to enable it to stand alone if taken out of context.

Profession Acting has long been known as The Profession. Not just as a profession but 'the' profession.

Programme (1) Sequence of performances scheduled for a theatre season. (2) Booklet giving information and credits for a performance. The scope may vary from a simple listing to a comprehensive book with detailed historical and illustrated analytical essays.

Projection (1) The ability of an actor to communicate nuances of a character's thoughts and emotions to an audience seated at a considerable distance from the stage. (2) Photographic or painted images projected on to screens or a scenic surface as part of a production's decor or scenography.

Prologue Speech or scene played prior to the first act.

Promenade Performance where the action shifts around a space shared by actors and audience. The audience are free to move around, following the action at floor level or observing from above. Promenade productions are particularly effective in theatres with a COURTYARD format.

Prompt Remind actors of the words when they forget.

Prompt Book (Copy) Master copy of the script or music score, containing all actor moves and technical cues, used by the stage management to control the performance.

Prompt Box Masked opening in the centre of the front edge of an opera stage to allow a prompter's head to be visible and audible to the performers.

Prompt Corner The position immediately behind the proscenium, traditionally on the actor's left side of the stage, from where the stage manager runs (ie controls) the performance by calling the cues. See **Bastard Prompt.**

Prompter In a play, the stage manager who runs the show is also responsible for prompting any actors who 'dry' (i.e. forget their words). But an opera is driven by the orchestra so, if a singer forgets a line, prompting after the dry is too late. Consequently every line has to be hissed out in advance by a member of the music staff from a little box in the centre of the footlights. But such prompting is now used in opera only when there has been limited rehearsals or an emergency cast change.

Props (Properties) Furnishings, set dressings and all items which cannot be classified as scenery or costumes.

Proscenium (Prosc, Pros. Arch) The division between audience and stage in the traditional form of theatre where the audience sits in a single block facing the stage. The proscenium takes many forms from a definte arch, not unlike a picture frame, to an unstressed termination of auditorium walls and ceiling.

Proscenium Doors Doors at the side of the stage, built into the proscenium of eighteenth century theatres. The actors normally made their entrances through these doors rather than through the scenery.

Provinces Older label for theatres outside London. Superseded by 'regional' which implies recognition of the importance of population centres outwith the capital.

P.S. Prompt side of the stage - actor's left when facing the audience. See **O.P.**

Public Virtually synonymous with audience. Certainly there is some tendency to refer to potential audience as 'the public'. Earlier generations of actors referred to their audience as 'my public', implying that the audience had come to see them rather than the play.

Pub Theatre A fringe performing space located in a room above or adjacent to the bar in a public house.

Puff An uncritical newspaper report designed to flatter a performer or production.

Pull To remove a ticket from a ticket book. Normally only done when the sale is confirmed and payment received. In computerised box offices, tickets are printed rather than pulled.

Punch Line Speech or part of a speech which emphasises or summarises the message of a scene.

Punters Audience are often referred to as punters in recognition of the risk involved in buying a ticket for a performance without knowing whether it will be enjoyable.

Put On Produce a production.

Q Normal way of writing **Cue.**

Quarter The call ('Quarter of an hour, please') given to warn actors that beginners will be called to the stage in fifteen minutes. Normally called twenty minutes before the advertised start time of the performance.

Queue In the days when gallery seating was unreserved, waiting in line was a key part of theatre experience for all ages of committed playgoers with small incomes. The niceties of proper behaviour had to be observed and were supervised by such characters as Winnie who rented folding stools to the galleryites for the Old Vic seasons at the New (now Albery) Theatre.

Quick Change An actor's fast change of costume.

Quick Study The ability to memorise a script quickly.

R

RADA Royal Academy of Dramatic Art.

Rag The house curtain.

Rake Inclined stage floor. To assist perspective, older stages had, and many have retained, a permanent rake rising by half an inch in each foot. (i.e. 1 in 24). Modern stages have a flat floor but many of today's scenic designs often include a temporary raked floor over part or all of the acting area.

Read Audition for a specific role, using the words of that role to assist the director to assess suitability for the role.

Read Through On the first day of rehearsal the cast usually sit in a circle and read their parts in a play. Most directors take the opportunity to precede the reading with a short explanation of the proposed production style and the designer shows the scale model of the scenery. Lighting and sound designers attend to meet the cast and listen to the reading to assist their understanding of the play.

Realism Totally real behaviour can never quite be achieved on a stage because communication with any but the very smallest audience requires at least a minimum strengthening of speech and movement, resulting in what is often called 'heightened reality'.

Real Pro An accolade by which colleagues acknowledge that an actor's behaviour, reliability and commitment are of the very highest standard.

Recall Invitation to attend a second audition for a part.

Recast Change some, or all, of the actors during a very long run. Few actors especially leading actors, wish to continue playing the same part every night after a year or even six months.

Receiving House A venue which does not have its own resident company of actors but presents packaged productions which have been prepared else-where - usually for a tour of several such receiving theatres. Consequently, a receiving theatre requires simpler stage facilties and administrative accomodation than a producing house.

Recitative The 'sung speech' of opera in which the plot is progressed between the 'songs' (arias) and 'sung ensembles' (duets, trios, quartets, quintets, sextets, choruses) in which the characters make comments on the emotional consequences of the storyline. Most recitative (recitativo secco) is accompanied by a **Continuo** of embellished chords played on a harpsichord with a cello optionally reinforcing the bass line. In the early operas of such pre-Mozart composers as Monteverdi and Handel the continuo often included lutes and organs.

Regional Theatres outside the capital city. Formerly known as provincial.

Regisseur Director.

Rehearse Prepare a performance. See **Dress Rehearsal, Technical Rehearsal.**

Rep Contraction of Repertory. Use of this contraction tends to imply an established ensemble of versatile actors prepared to play a very wide range of roles.

Repertoire A theatre organisation where two or more productions alternate in the course of a week's performances. See **Stagione**.

Repertory A theatre, usually with a permanent company of actors, where each production has a run of limited length. At any time there is normally one production in performance, another in rehearsal, and several in various degrees of preparation.

Repetiteur Pianist and vocal coach in an opera house.

Reprise Music from an earlier scene repeated in shortened form. A musical device used to link events, particularly when dreams of love become reality.

Resident A theatre company or individual staff members who are attached to a theatre on a long-term basis, probably open-ended.

Residency Arrangement whereby a company is based for a season in a theatre, not just performing but having a community involvement with classes, workshops, etc.

Resolution Final part of the plot when the various intricacies are unravelled and the conflicts explained with consequences which vary from the living happily ever after of a comedy, through the arrests of a whodunnit, to the inevitable doom of a tragedy.

Resting Euphemism for being out of work. See **At Liberty**.

Restoration The surge in the development of English dramatic writing and performance between the coronation of Charles II in 1600 and the end of the century.

Resume A summary of an actor's professional training and performing experience. (Mostly US.)

Return (1) A statement of ticket sales produced by the box office manager nightly, and summarised weekly. (2) A subsidiary scenic flat set at right angles to a more important flat, usually to complete the masking of the scene.

Revamp A rethink of one or more aspects of a production.

Review A media report of a production, offering a critical assessment of the quality of its writing, interpretation and performance.

Revival (1) Re-creation of an older production for which the original scenery and costumes have been in storage. This type of revival is common in opera and normally includes reproducing the basic interpretation and moves since these tend to be constrained by the original scenography. (2) A completely new production of a piece which has not been performed for some time.

Revolve A turntable in the stage floor. Used for scene changing or as a production device where the actors walk, dance or even bicycle against the direction of rotation.

Revue A production compiled from a series of musical and comedy items.

Rhubarb The traditional word which actors mutter in crowd scenes to make the rumbling sound of conversation. Consequently the word is sometimes also used for verbal rubbish.

Right Actor's right, facing the audience. See O.P.

Rights Legal authority to perform a work as a result of ownership of the copyright or possession of a licence from the copyright holder.

Ring Up/Down Cueing the curtain up and down, particularly at the start and end of the performance. In the eighteenth century, the prompter gave the cue by a bell which could often be heard by the audience.

Rise The beginning of the performance (at the rise of the curtain).

RNT ROYAL NATIONAL THEATRE

Road (1) On tour. (2) In US, the entire nation outside New York City.

Role A person portrayed by an actor in a play.

Rolling in the Aisles So funny that the audience sitting next to the aisles fall (at least, metaphorically) off their seats with laughter. See **Not a Dry Eye in the House, Not a Dry Seat in the House.**

Roscius An actor. Derived from the Roman actor Quintus Roscius Gallus.

Rough Theatre A performance style which is more concerned with developing rapport with the audience by a broad, apparently unpolished, attacking approach rather than by attempting to formalise the more delicate nuances of human behaviour. Peter Brook has drawn attention to the imperfections or 'roughness' in all human activity.

Round Applause, particularly that given to an actor during the course of performance. See also **Theatre in the Round.**

Routine (1) A dance sequence. (2) A variety act, particularly one involving visual comedy.

Royal Circle A balcony, usually the lowest one offering the best seating (i.e. an alternative name to Grand Circle or Dress Circle) but occasionally used to upgrade the marketing image of the second best balcony.

Royal National Theatre Britain's national theatre for drama was established at the Old Vic in 1963 and moved into its three theatre building on the South Bank in 1976. In 1988 it became the Royal National Theatre.

Royalty Payment made in respect of copyright to an author, composer, director, choreographer or designer. Normally a percentage of box office receipts, although it may be a fixed sum for each performance.

RSC Royal Shakespeare Company.

Run A sequence of performances of the same production.

Running Time The length of a scene, act or performance. Running times of each performance are carefully recorded by the stage manager since changes provide a good monitor of any departure from the original pace. Allowance has to be made for differing audience responses: a comedy played to a Saturday full house will take longer than at a mid-week matinee.

Run of the Play Contracted to act a role for as long as audience interest justifies the production continuing.

Run Out A platform over the orchestra pit with steps down to the auditorium. Sometimes used to allow actors to address the audience or to enter from the auditorium in performance, but more frequently for the production team to have access to the stage from the auditorium during rehearsals.

Run Through A rehearsal where the emphasis is on continuity. The actors try to keep going by ignoring small problems for which they or the director would normally stop.

Runway Narrow extension of the stage - either around the orchestra pit or part way up the centere aisle or both - primarily for dancers in revue and vaudeville.

S

Safety Curtain Fire resistant curtain designed to contain a fire within the stage area of a proscenium theatre in order to gain time for the audience to escape.

Scalper A seller of tickets at inflated prices for performances which are sold out at the box office.

Scenario A synopsis of the plot and characters, with an outline of the scene-by-scene sequence of events.

Scene (1) A segment of a play, usually comprising events contained within a block of time which is seperate from the events preceeding and following. (2) The visual stage environment designed to support an acting performance.

Scenographer A designer of sets, costumes or lights which are an integral part of the production concept.

Scenography The international term for all aspects of design where the visual environment is an integral part of the production concept rather than just a decorative background.

Score The music for a performance, particularly its written notation. The 'full score' includes staves for each of the individual instrumental parts.

Scottish Play, The Unless actually working on a production of Macbeth, it is considered unlucky to mention the play on the stage or in the dressing room. This superstition probably arises from the number of accidents which have occurred in rehearsals and performances.

Script The text of a play.

Season A series of productions played within a specific period of time, probably marketed together as a group, and possibly performed by the same acting company.

Segue Musical term for one number to follow another without a break. Used in theatre to indicate immediate continuity of all kinds, sometimes with emphasis provided by the qualification "dead segue".

Sell Out Performance, or season, for which all seats have been sold.

Send Up Extract humour from ideas or characters by treating them with exaggerated seriousness. On the stage, as in life, the individual or institution may not realise, at least initially, that they are being 'sent up'.

Set Often used as a synonym for "scenery", although there is some implication of a substantial structure, much of which may be permanent for the duration of the performance.

Shares Dividing the box-office receipts, less expenses, as an alternative to paying salaries. An old practice almost, but not totally, extinct.

Shelf Theatre circles and balconies are often referred to as shelves, especially by comedians when addressing the audience directly. See **Ashtrays.**

Show General word for any performance, but particularly one which includes more than just spoken dialogue.

Show Biz A romantic view of the theatre industry. As Annie Oakley sang 'There's No Business Like Show Business'. To which a cynic might reply 'which is lucky for the other businesses'.

Showcase A performance organised for the specific purpose of giving the performers an opportunity of demonstrating their skills and talents to an audience of people who may be able to employ them.

Showgirl Dancer who moves elegantly and poses in exotic costumes which are designed to expose and enhance the contours of the human figure. Showgirls feature as a mainly scenographic element in light entertainment productions.

Show Must Go On A tradition, and a saying, that encapsulates the theatre world's determination to give an advertised performance despite adverse circumstances of any kind. That this aim is consistently achieved is quite remarkable in view of the fact that dates are announced, and tickets sold, for plays while they are still in the process of being written, designed and cast.

Show Report A document, completed for each performance, in which the stage manager records running times, any problems such as missed cues, audience response and the number of curtain calls.

Showstopper A song or production number which generates such applause that the performance is temporarily brought to a halt.

Sightline Extent of visibility of the stage from any particular seat, especially from such extreme seats as those in front and back rows, at the sides, and in galleries.

Sit on Their Hands An audience who are less than generous with their applause.

Site Specific A production which has been conceived for performance in a particular environmental space rather than a conventional theatre.

Sitzprobe Opera rehearsal, with orchestra, where the cast sing but do not act.

Sketch A short self-contained scene, usually comedy, in a revue or variety production.

Skin Act An actor or pair of actors wearing a realistic costume to impersonate an animal.

Skip A large strong wicker basket used to transport costumes and props.

Slap Make-up.

Slapstick Pair of thin timber laths, separated at the handle by a spacer, traditionally used by clowns as a weapon which makes a noise without hurting. Still used in schoolroom scenes of Christmas pantomimes. Origin of the type of humour bearing the name.

Slips Side gallery seating from which there is only a partial or even negligible view of the stage.

Slosh Comedy scenes, mainly associated with Christmas pantomime, involving encounters between actors and wet viscous mixtures. These scenes usually involve making custard pies in a kitchen or wallpapering a room. Traditional slosh is made by whisking shaving soap, water and colouring. There are few higher backstage skills than mixing slosh to perfect consistency, and its use is the prime test of any comedian's timing.

Smell of the Greasepaint A romantic phrase which conjures up the aromatic component of backstage atmosphere. The other, often more persistent, odour was that of SIZE. But both have been supplanted by the bland fragrances of new technology.

Soliloquy A solo speech, delivered as if thinking aloud, in which a character shares thoughts with the audience but not with the other characters in the play.

SOLT Society of London Theatre. An association of theatre managers and producers responsible for nurturing London theatre, particularly in the west end. They protect and promote their members' interests by lobbying, negotiating with unions, and marketing.

Song Sheet A flown rectangle of cloth painted with the words of a song which the audience are invited to join in singing. Still traditionally used by the star in virtually every Christmas pantomime as part of the frontcloth scene which covers the change into spectacular scenery and costumes for the finale.

Soubrette Actress specialising in vivacious comedy roles, usually involving the kind of intrigue that is indigenous to the lifestyle of the pert maid servants of the operatic world and their saucy sisters in musical comedy.

Spear Carrier A young Shakespearean actor who plays very small parts with an occasional line and generally helps to dress the stage.

Speciality A self-contained act, usually involving special, even bizarre, skills. Speciality acts include jugglers, acrobats, contortionists, mind readers, impressionists, ventriloquists and players of concertos on a garden hose connected to a kitchen sink - a whole series of performing skills which have become obsolescent with the decline of variety and vaudeville.

Speciality Music Much of the music played by pit bands to accompany speciality acts was cheerfully bland rum-ti-tum and rarely seemed to be particularly relevant to the act. Its most significant features were the cues to play softly while something difficult was attempted and loudly when it was achieved. For particular feats of daring or dexterity, the music would stop and be replaced by drum rolls followed by loud chords to stimulate applause.

Spelvin See **George Spelvin.**

Spike To mark, with paint or coloured tape, the position of scenery or furniture on the stage.

Split week A week in which a touring company plays more than one venue.

Sponsorship Funding provided by commercial businesses rather than by central or local government. It is a form of advertising with the sponsoring firm seeking to enhance its image by community involvement.

Spot (1) The position of an act in the running order of a variety bill. (2) An opportunity in a revue or Christmas pantomime for an actor to insert a short solo sequence of singing, dancing or comedy. (3) A spotlight.

Stage, The A newspaper, published weekly in London on Thursdays since 1880. It is devoted to news for show business professionals and carries adverts for theatre jobs.

Stage Crew Technicians responsible for scenery handling.

Stage Directions Playwright's suggestions which supplement the dialogue in a script.

Stage Director Formerly the senior member of the stage management team but a title now rarely used in order to avoid confusion with the director.

Stage Door Johnny An upper class admirer of actresses, particularly chorus girls, in the era of the Edwardian theatre.

Stage Door Keeper See **Hallkeeper.**

Stage Fright Even the most established actor can experience a fear of going on to the stage and facing the audience. Indeed some anxiety is almost inevitable as a result of the inherently sensitive nature of an actor's temperament. Although stage fright most commonly results from the insecurity of a first performance, it can strike unexpectedly during a long run.

Stagehand Technician who handles scenery.

Stage Manager The person in overall control of the performance with responsibility for signalling the cues that co-ordinate the work of the actors and technicians. Some of this responsibility is delegated to the deputy stage manager (DSM) and assistant stage manager (ASM).

Stage Name An actor may adopt a professional name at the beginning of their career to avoid confusion with an actor who is already established. Or they may feel that their career prospects would improve by selecting a name which might be more memorably distinctive in speech and print.

Stage Wait An interruption to the flow of the performance caused by an actor 'drying' or being 'off', or by a problem with a scene change.

Stage Whisper An actor speaking as if whispering, but in a way that can still be heard by the audience.

Stagey Very artificial.

Stagger Through An early attempt at continuity when segments which have been rehearsed seperately are run in sequence. An early **Run Through.**

Staging The process of preparing and performing a dramatic work.

Stagione A form of repertoire with a very limited range of productions in performance during any particular period. Each production is given intense rehearsal followed by a short group of performances close together although not on adjacent evenings. Revivals are re-rehearsed almost as if they were new productions.

Stalls Audience seating at ground floor level. Originally just a few comfortable seats introduced at the front of the pit benches but gradually taking over the entre area. (ORCHESTRA in US.)

Stand Up Comic Comedian who performs solo, talking directly to the audience without support from feeds, stooges or straight men.

Stanislavski Russian actor and director who reacted against the conventional histrionics of the late 19th and early 20th centuries by advocating an acting style based on natural sincerity. His insistence on the need to build a character from within rather than by superimposition of external mannerisms remains a major influence.

Star A well known and charismatic actor capable of attracting an audience, many of whom can be expected to buy tickets irrespective of the title of the production.

Star Trap A small square trap, just large enough to allow an actor to be speedily projected on a counterweighted platform through the stage from below. The surface is cut into small hinged triangular sections in the shape of a star which open as the actor passes through, then immediately fall back into place.

Star Vehicle A show structured to display the talents of a particular star performer.

Steal An actor contriving to become the focus of a scene ('steal the scene') even if this threatens to distort a balanced interpretation of the dramatist's intentions.

Sting A shimmering musical chord to emphasise a moment of magic.

Stock (1) Formerly, in UK, a resident company performing a series of plays in repertoire. (2) Now, in US, a resident company performing a series of plays in repertory.

Stooge Similar to the **Straight Man** who **Feeds** a comedian. However a stooge tends to be rather more of a target for the comedian's jokes.

Straight Non-musical, as in straight play or straight actor.

Straight Man The serious half of a comedy double act. The straight man (who may well be a woman) feeds a sequence of serious lines to the comedian who responds with the funny lines which raise the laughs.

Strike Dismantling a scene and removing it, and/or props, from the acting area.

Stripper Actor who entertains by removing items of clothing in a provocative manner to a musical accompaniment. Strippers were once almost exclusively female, but male stripping has recently increased in popularity.

Strutt Act - as in Shakespeare's 'poor player that struts and frets his hour upon the stage' (Macbeth).

Stub The portion of a ticket retained by the box office for accounting purposes.

Studio Small flexible performance space associated with experimental productions.

Study Preparation of an acting role, particularly the memorising of the lines.

Sub Plot A subsidiary storyline which interweaves with the main plot.

Subsidy With the exception of long running popular plays and musicals, box office income is insufficient to meet the costs of operating a theatre. Apart from audience resistance to high seat prices, access to the arts is accepted as a desirable feature of a civilised society. This places theatres in the same category as museums, art galleries and libraries which require funding support from national and local government budgets.

Sub Text Ideas and emotions inferred by the play but not stated in its dialogue.

Summer Stock US term for companies playing summer seasons.

Super Contraction of supernumerary. An extra actor, with no dialogue, who helps fills up the stage, particularly in crowd scenes.

Superstitions No real flowers on the stage, no whistling in the dressing room, no mention of Macbeth .... the list is endless, almost meriting an ABC of Theatre Superstition!

Support The actor or actors who perform with a star.

Suspension of Disbelief Audience acceptance of performance conventions as reality.

SWET Society of West End Theatre, which was formerly SWETM (Society of West End Theatre Management) and has now become SOLT. (SWET and SWETM were rather unfortunate acronyms for managements wishing to project a caring image!)

T

Tableaux A picture formed by a group of motionless actors. When house curtains were more popular than they are now, the device was often used at the beginnings and ends of acts.

Tabs (1) Originally 'tableaux curtains' which drew outwards and upwards, but now generally applied to any curtain, including vertically flying front curtains (e.g. house tabs) and, especially, a pair of horizontally moving curtains which move outwards from a centre overlap. (2) Music to accompany the acknowledgement of applause at end of a variety act.

Tag A line of dialogue or an action which marks the climax of a scene or a sequence within that scene. When the tag is a joke, it is often the cue for a blackout.

Take (1) A momentary but significant facial reaction. See **Double Take.** (2) Assume a commanding position as in 'take the stage' or 'take centre'.

Take Direction The willingness and ability of an actor to respond positively to suggestions made by the director.

Tatty Standards of presentation rather less than spick and span.

Techie An increasingly used contraction for technician.

Text The words of a play.

Theatregoers People who attend performances on a regular basis.

Theatre-in-the-Round Staging format where the audience encircles the acting area

Theatre of the Absurd See **Absurd, Theatre of.**

Theatre of Cruelty See **Cruelty, Theatre of.**

The Boys The stage crew, particularly the crew, including casuals, who work the performances in a touring theatre. Dying out with the growth of gender equality.

There's No Business Like Show Business Song from the Irving Berlin musical 'Annie Get Your Gun' which has become a clichéd anthem for the glitzier aspects of theatre. See **Show Biz.**

Thespian An actor. Derived from 'Thespis', the classical Greek poet who first added a solo actor to the chorus.

Throw Away A line which the actor delivers without emphasis or meaning.

Throwaway A small advertising leaflet. See **Flier.**

Thrust A stage which projects into the auditorium so that the audience are seated on at least two sides.

Tie Theatre-in-Education. A group of actors, usually attached to a regional playhouse, who tour play performances to schools.

Timing Responding to words or events by speaking a line or making a gesture at precisely the right moment to convey maximum meaning to an audience. Timing is a very sensitive reaction to the response of each audience, especially in comedy. It is particularly concerned with barely discernible variations in the length of pauses. See **Beat, Pace.**

Toi Toi Toi Theatre superstition rejects the use of phrases such as 'Good Luck'. Spitting over the shoulder is a preferred gesture in the operatic world, although in the interests of hygiene (and singers are justifiably paranoid about their throats) the spitting is usually formalised into the words 'Toi Toi Toi'.

Tony The Broadway theatre's most prestigious award. Named after 1930s actress-director Antoinette Perry.

Top and Tail Cutting out the dialogue and action between technical cues in a rehearsal.

Top of the Bill The most important performer in an evening of variety. Occupies the highest position on the poster and presents the final act of the evening as the climax of the performance.

Tour A production taken to a sequence of theatres in different towns. Mainstream tours traditionally spend a week or multiple of a week in each theatre. See **Bus and Truck, Road.**

Toy Theatres See **Paper Theatres.**

Tragedy A serious play which moves inevitably towards disastrous, usually fatal, consequences for the central character.

Train Call Departure time when, in the heyday of the railways, all touring theatre companies travelled by train and the actors were required to travel as a group in a reserved coach in order to qualify for free wagons for the scenery.

Transfer Moving a production from a regional or fringe theatre to the West End. Or from one West End theatre to another one.

Transformation A magical scene change where one scene melts into another. Often effected by exploiting the varying transparency of gauze under different lighting conditions, or by the instant swivelling of scenery.

Trap Section of stage floor which can be opened for access to and from the understage area, often called "trap room" or "cellar". Standard equipment of older stages included a central grave trap and corner traps with mechanism to project actors through the stage floor at speed. See **Star Trap.**

Traverse (1) A form of staging where the audience sit on two sides of the stage - so that the stage runs through the audience. (2) A curtain that runs across the stage.

Tread the Boards Act in a theatre.

Treasury A call for paying weekly salaries, traditionally held on Fridays. With improvements in the financial stability of theatre companies (or at least in the indemnities protecting their employees) and the growing sophistication of the banking system, the traditional treasury call is tending to be replaced by direct credit transfers.

Troupe A group of performers who work regularly together.

Trouper An actor, particularly one who has experienced years of touring discomfort, even hardship, but remains cheerful and takes pride in behaving in a very professional manner.

Try Out (1) A production of a new play to discover its strengths and weaknesses, particularly in terms of audience response, with a view to possible re-writing if necessary. (2) Touring a new production to fine-tune it before presenting on Broadway or London's West End.

Tuppence Coloured See **Penny Plain, Tuppence Coloured.**

Turkey A production which fails to impress, particularly at the box office.

Turn A self-contained act in a Variety Bill.

Typecasting (1) Casting a play by choosing actors who closely resemble the physical and personality characteristics of each role. (2) Casting actors in roles similar to ones that they have already played successfully. Such type casting also tends to extend to directors and designers.

Twofer Two tickets for the price of one. A marketing device used particularly for Monday nights on tour and for shows which are in the final weeks of long runs.

U

Uber Marionette Edward Gordon Craig's proposal for an actor who, rather than display emotional involvement, would peform like a formalised puppet manipulated by the director in a production style motivated primarily by visual rather than by textual considerations.

Underplay To act with less than expected emphasis on words and movement.

Underscore Music played under dialogue, usually when speech is leading into song in a musical.

Understudy Actor who stands by to take over the role of a member of the cast unable to perform due to illness. Opera understudies are usually called **Covers.**

Up Performance start time as in 'When do we go up?', 'We go up at 8.30.', 'We went up at 8.35.' See DOWN (2).

Upper Circle A highish balcony, usually above the Grand or Dress Circle but below the Gallery.

Upstage The part of the stage furthest from the audience.

Upstaging An actor dominating a scene by moving upstage so that other actors are forced to turn away from the audience.

Use the Stage Take command of the stage, making broad sweeping movements around the central acting area.

V

Vamp Spring loaded flap in scenery which closes immediately an actor has made an entrance through it.

Vamp 'Til Ready Music repeated or extemporised to cover a break in continuity caused by waiting until a scene change has been completed or an actor makes a delayed entrance.

Variety (1) A traditional variety performance, known as a variety bill, comprises a sequence of acts which follow each other without any linking material between them. There may be one or several performers in each act which is a self-contained mini-production with its own script, music, costumes and props. The scenery is usually cloths and drapes from the venue theatre's stock. (2) US weekly newspaper for film, television and theatre giving news and box-office receipts.

Vaudeville The US equivalent of **Variety.**

Vehicle A play which has been selected, or even written, because it will provide an opportunity to display the talents of a particular actor or company.

Venue Any place where a performance can take place.

Vomitory Auditorium entrance, tunnelled through the seating tiers. Also used by actors for entrances to thrust stages and theatres-in-the-round. Often shortened to 'Voms' in conversation.

W

Walk On A subsidiary role played by a non-speaking actor.

Walk Down The last scene of a revue or Christmas pantomime when the actors enter one by one to take their applause. The scene is usually spectacularly designed with a central staircase so that each performer, wearing a costume not previously seen in the show, can make an impressive entrance. After the individual bows, the cast line up along the front of the stage to sing a final musical number.

Walk It (1) Give a superficial performance by making the moves and speaking the dialogue without interpreting or projecting the role. A technique sometimes used towards the end of a long detailed technical rehearsal. (2) A critical term used to describe a shallow performance.

Walter Plinge Name used on posters and programmes printed before the role is cast. Sometimes also used when an actor is playing ('doubling') two roles. See **George Spelvin.**

Wardrobe General name for the costume department, its staff, and the accommodation that they occupy.

Warm Up Gradual exercise by singers and dancers to prepare their voices and limbs prior to rehearsal or performance. The purpose is not just to sing and dance well but to protect delicate vocal chords and leg muscles from damage.

Week Out A week in the middle of a tour when performances are suspended because no suitable theatre is available.

Weekly Rep A resident drama company rehearsing and performing each play for one week. The strain of performing every night, rehearsing every morning and memorising every afternoon, week after week, makes it impossible to sustain standards which are acceptable to either actors or audience. Weekly rep was killed off by the higher production standards of television and the normal rehearsal period gradually became two, three and four weeks. See **Repertoire** and **Repertory.**

Well Made Play A logically structured plot with such clarity of exposition, development and resolution that few, if any, uncertainties remain to challenge the audience imagination.

West End London's commercial theatre district, centred around Shaftesbury Avenue, Charing Cross Road, St Martin's Lane and The Strand.

Wet White Liquid make-up used for covering non-facial parts of the body.

Whitehall Farce From the 1950s to the 1970s, under the direction of Brian Rix (now Lord Rix), London's Whitehall Theatre was the home to a highly successful series of farces which explored traditional misunderstandings concerning lost trousers within the context of contemporary life styles. See **Aldwych Farce.**

Whodunnit A play about a crime, usually a murder, carried out by someone whose identity forms the denouement. Confronted by a series of possibilities, the audience spend the evening speculating about who committed the crime. The detective is a pivotal acting role and there is a considerable degree of silent audience participation as everyone tries to assess motives, weigh evidence and unravel false trails. The most famous whodunnit is Agatha Christie's 'Mousetrap' which has been running continuously in London since 1952. By now everybody knows who 'dun' this particular 'it', but it would be irresponsible to name the villain here!

Wings (1) The technical areas to the sides of the acting area. (2) Scenery standing where the acting area joins these technical areas.

Wing a Part Performing a role without having fully memorised the words. The phrase is derived from keeping a script off stage (in the 'wings') for consultation between entrances, although more desperate measures have been known to include pinning pages of script to scenery or concealing them on furniture.

Word of Mouth A show which receives good publicity by audiences telling their friends how much they have enjoyed the performance. In the spirit of optimism with which actors and theatres rate their audience appeal, it rarely seems to occur to anyone, and is certainly not to be mentioned, that word of mouth can also work in a negative way.

Worked (Name of Theatre or town) Performed at that theatre or town.

Work the Show Be a member of the technical crew for a performance.

Workshopping Rehearsing an idea or an incomplete script in order to explore and develop its dramatic possibilities.

X, Y, Z

X Notation for actor positions in prompt scripts.

Yes? An actor's way of asking for a prompt during rehearsals.

Zarzuela Spanish musical form similar to operetta.

ENTERTAINMENT TECHNOLOGY PRESS

FREE SUBSCRIPTION SERVICE

Keeping Up To Date with

The ABC of Theatre Jargon

Entertainment Technology Press titles are continually up-dated, and all changes and additions are listed in date order in the relevant dedicated area of the publisher's website. Simply go to the front page of www.etnow.com and click on the BOOKS button. From there you can locate the title and be connected through to the latest information related to this publication.

Francis Reid welcomes corrections to existing entries in this book and suggestions for new ones, which can be added to later editions of the title on a regular basis. He can be contacted at: francisreid@btinternet.com